Luis Fernando Aguas Bucheli

Mastering Object Oriented Programming with Java in NetBeans

Luis Fernando Aguas Bucheli

Mastering Object Oriented Programming with Java in NetBeans

Complete Guide to Laboratory Practices with Aguaszoft

ScienciaScripts

Cover image: www.ingimage.com

This book is a translation from the original published under ISBN 978-620-2-14896-2.

Publisher:
Sciencia Scripts
is a trademark of
Dodo Books Indian Ocean Ltd. and OmniScriptum S.R.L publishing group

120 High Road, East Finchley, London, N2 9ED, United Kingdom
Str. Armeneasca 28/1, office 1, Chisinau MD-2012, Republic of Moldova, Europe
Printed at: see last page
ISBN: 978-620-8-24649-5

Contents

PRACTICE 1

1. **TOPIC:** JAVA Basics
2. **OBJECTIVES:**
- Acquire the basic concepts related to OOP.
- Recognise the characteristics of the OOP
3. **SUSTAINABLE DEVELOPMENT GOALS:**

Indicator 4.7: By 2030, ensure that all learners acquire the knowledge and skills needed to promote sustainable development, including through education for sustainable development and sustainable lifestyles, human rights, gender equality, promotion of a culture of peace and non-violence, global citizenship and appreciation of cultural diversity and the contribution of culture to sustainable development

4. **INTRODUCTION:**

Java is a general-purpose, object-oriented, typed, object-oriented programming language, which allows the development of applications ranging from basic applications, through enterprise applications to mobile applications.

Java was born as a programming language that could be cross-platform and multi-device, under the "Write Once Run Anywhere" (WORA) paradigm.

In this way a Java program written once can be run on different platforms, being supported on Windows, MacOs and UNIX operating systems. And in turn on different types of devices.

In order to follow this paradigm, the compilation of a Java program does not generate source code, but generates bytecodes. These bytecodes are interpreted by a virtual machine or JVM (Java Virtual Machine). This machine is already written for each of the operating systems in question.

Java language features

Among the features of the Java language we find:

Platform Independent

When compiling Java source code, no specific machine code is generated, but bytecodes are generated, which are interpreted by the Java Virtual Machine (JVM), making it possible for the same source code to be executed on multiple platforms.

Object Oriented

Any element of the Java language is an object. Within objects, data is encapsulated, which is accessed by mëtodos.

Simple

Java is intended to be an easy language to learn. You simply need to understand the basic concepts of object-oriented programming (OOP).

Insurance

It is secure because programs run inside the Java Virtual Machine (JVM) in a "sandbox" format, so they cannot access anything outside of it.

It has a validation on the bytecodes to check for illegal fragment codes.

Neutral Architecture

Regardless of whether it runs on 32bit or 64bit architecture. In Java, data types always take up the same amount of space.

Portable

Java has no platform dependencies, which makes it portable to different platforms.

Robust

The Java language attempts to control error situations in the compilation and execution processes, thus reducing the risk of failure.

In addition, Java takes full control of memory by allocating and removing it through a garbage collector, so that we cannot use pointers to access it.

Multi-thread

Java allows concurrent programming, so that a single program can open different threads.

Interpreted

The bytecodes are interpreted in real time to machine code.

High Performance

Java offers Just-In-Time compilers that allow for high performance.

Distributed

The Java language is intended to run on distributed architectures, such as the Internet.

5. DEVELOPMENT:

"Netbeans login

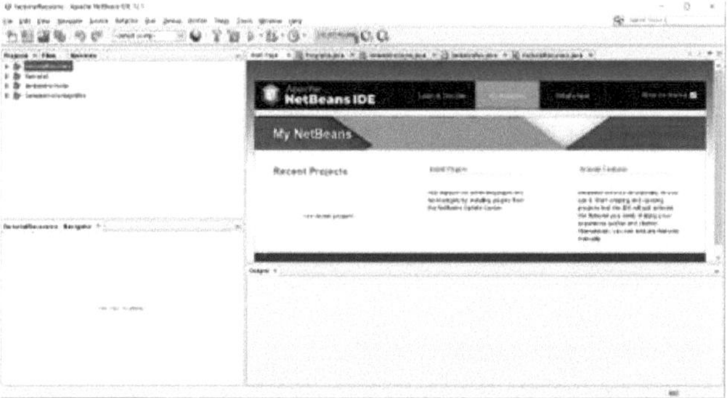

"We created a new project:

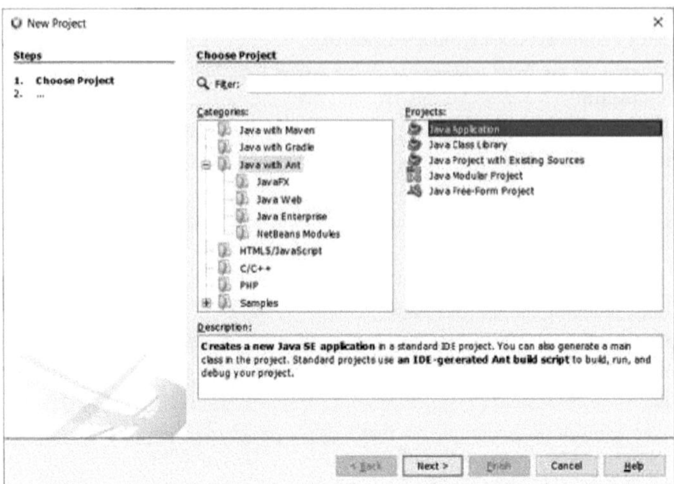

"We place as name

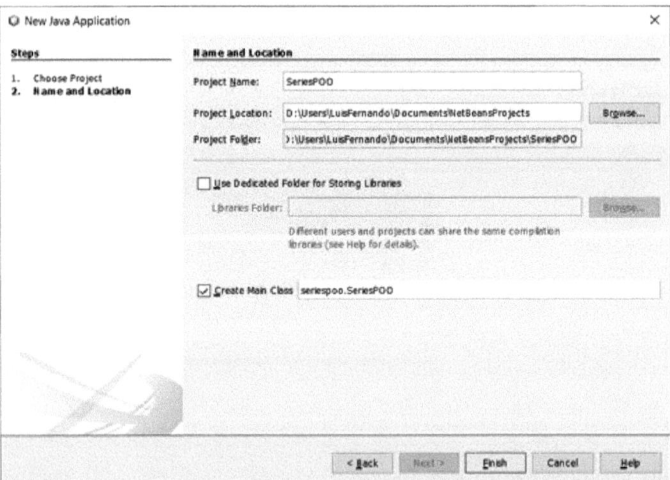

Click on finalizer

Delete the SeriesPOO.java file

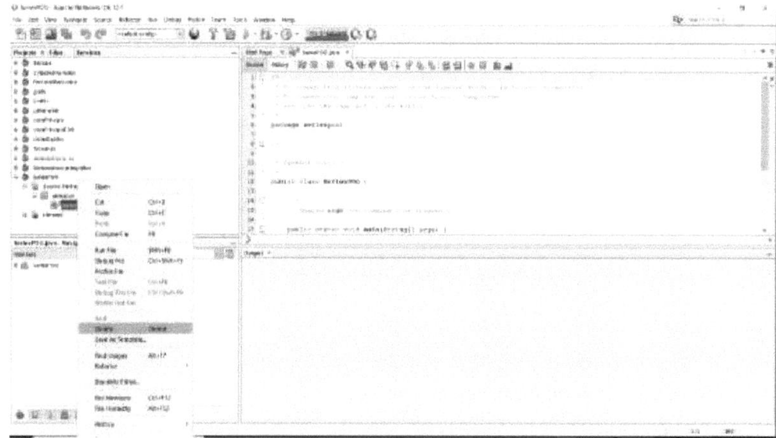

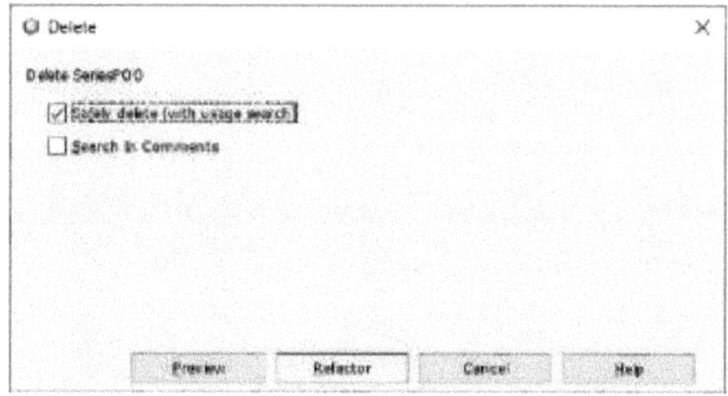

Then click on Refactor

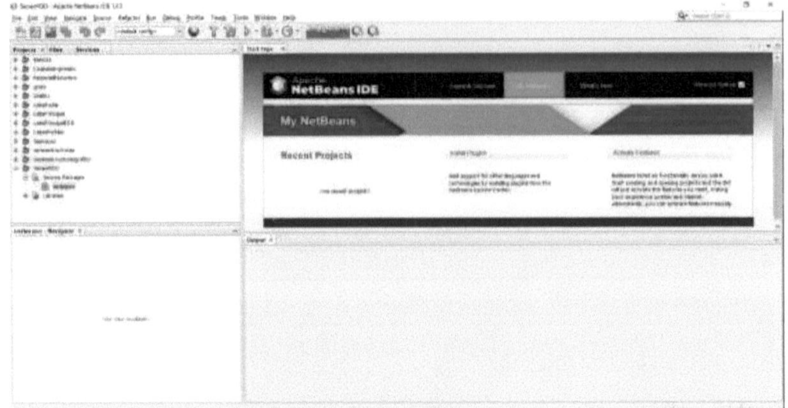

Right click on the SeriesPOO package and add a JFrame.

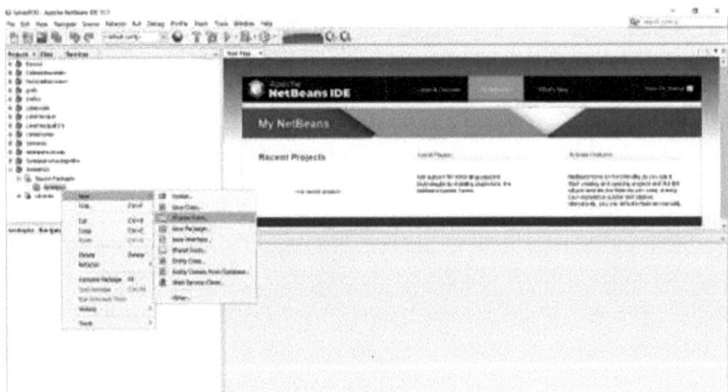

Enter the following name and then click on finalizer

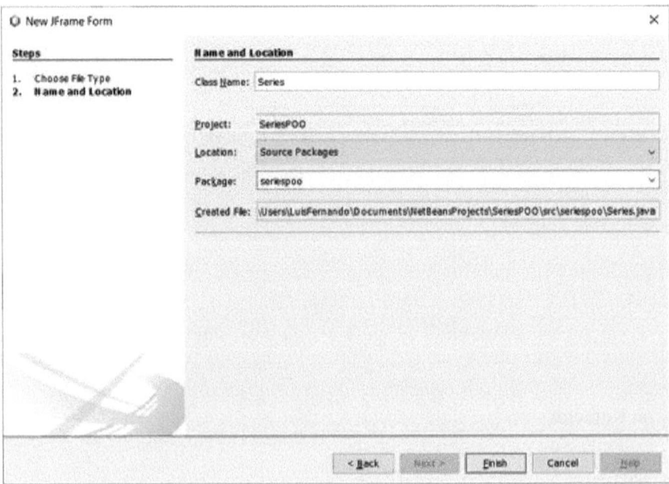

Having:

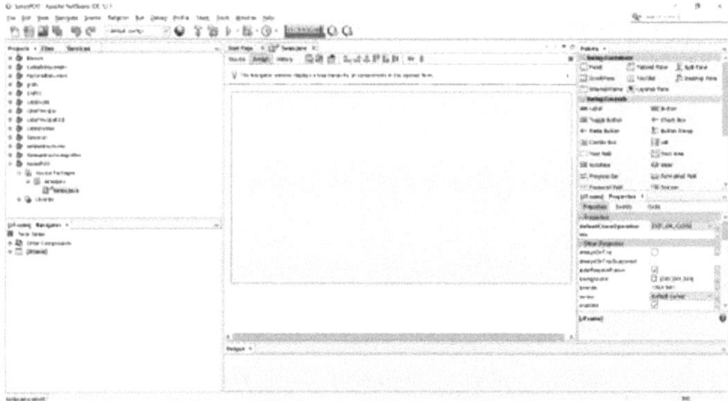

Click on the JFrame and in properties, in title we write: Series

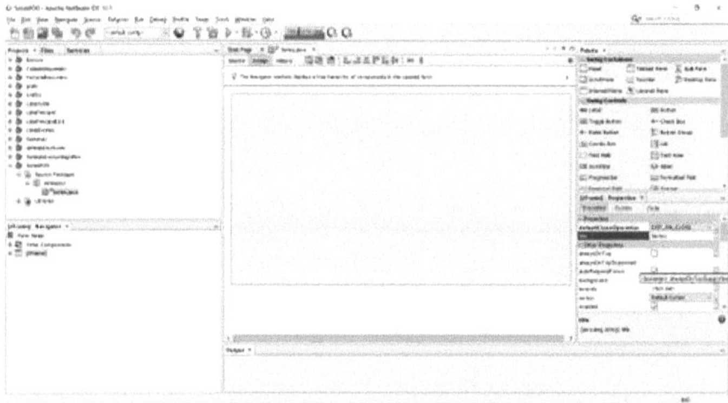

We are going to make 4 basic series: even, odd, prime and Fibonacci.

For peers:

Select a jPanel from the palette and in the jPanel place a jLabel, a jButton, a jTextArea in the following manner

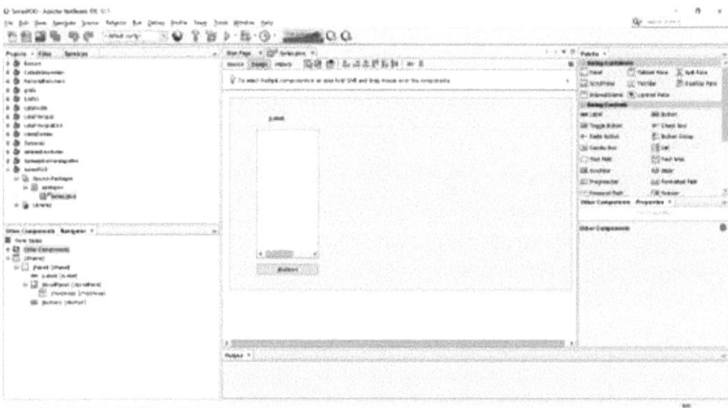

Click on jLabel and go to the text property and enter the following:

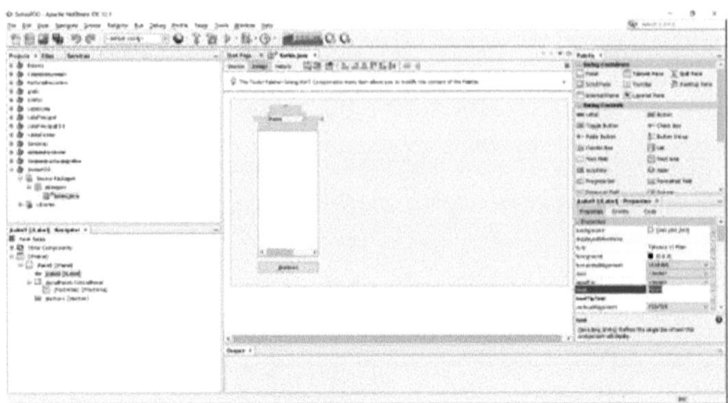

Click on the jButton and go to properties and set text:

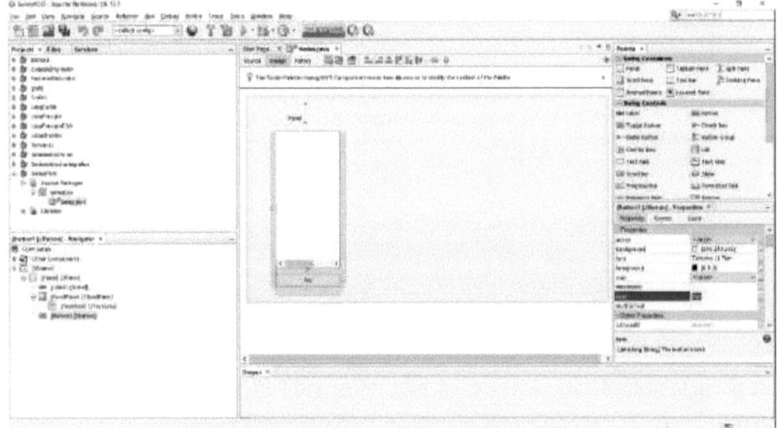

Double click on the JButton, to activate the click event, place the following code

```
private void jButton1ActionPerformed(java.awt.event.ActionEvent evt) { for (int i = 0; i <=
20; i++)
jTextArea1.append("\n" + i * 2);
```

Having:

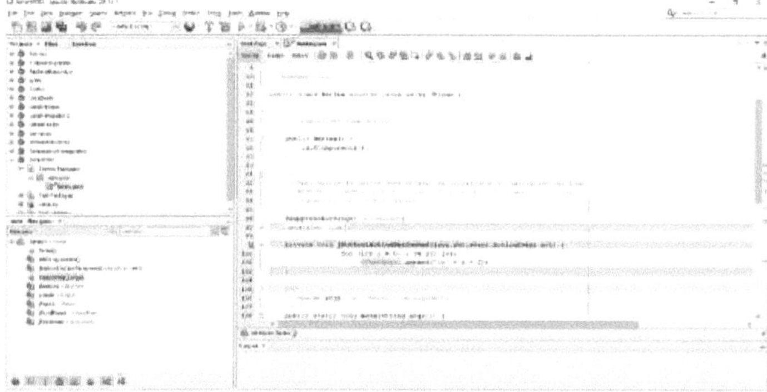

Click on compile and then on run

For odd numbers:

We select from the palette, a jPanel and in the jPanel we place jLabel, a jButton, a jTextArea and we do the same process as above:

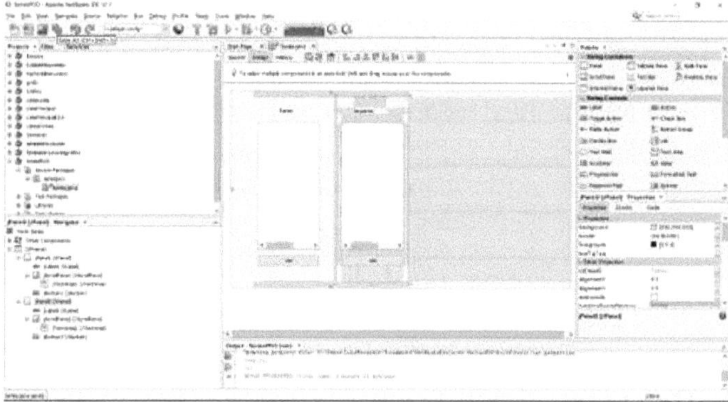

Double click on the JButton, to activate the click event, we place the following code private void jButton2ActionPerformed(java.awt.event.ActionEvent evt) { { {

for (int i = 0; i <= 20; i++) jTextArea2.append("\n" +(2*i +1)); }

Having:

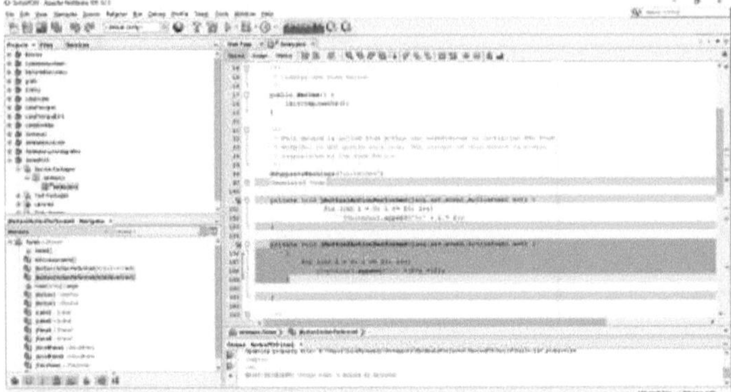

Click on compile and then on run

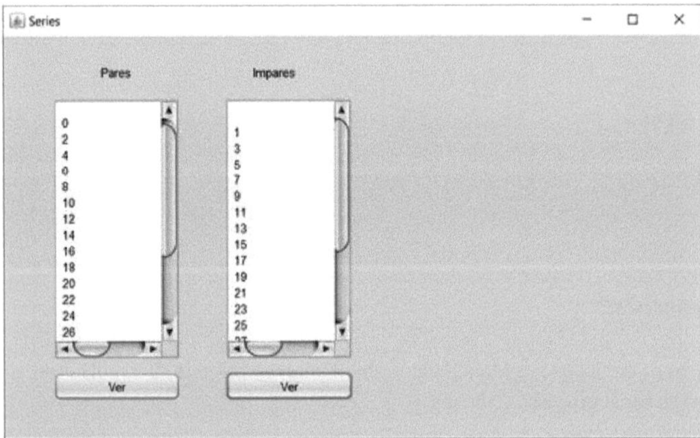

For the fibonacci:
We select from the palette, a jPanel and in the jPanel we place a jLabel, a jButton, a jTextArea and we do the same process as above:

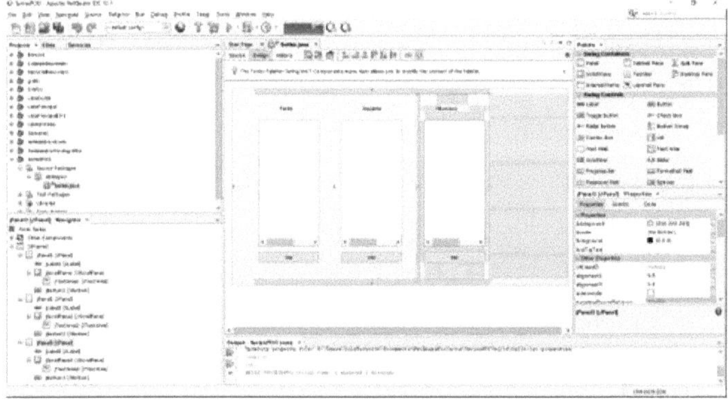

Double click on the JButton, to activate the click event, place the following code

```
private void jButton3ActionPerformed(java.awt.event.ActionEvent evt) {
int f = 0;
int t1 = 1;
int t2;
for (int i = 1; i <= 20; i++)
{
t2 = f;
f = t1 + f;
t1 = t2;
jTextArea3.append("\n" + t1);
}
}
```

Having:

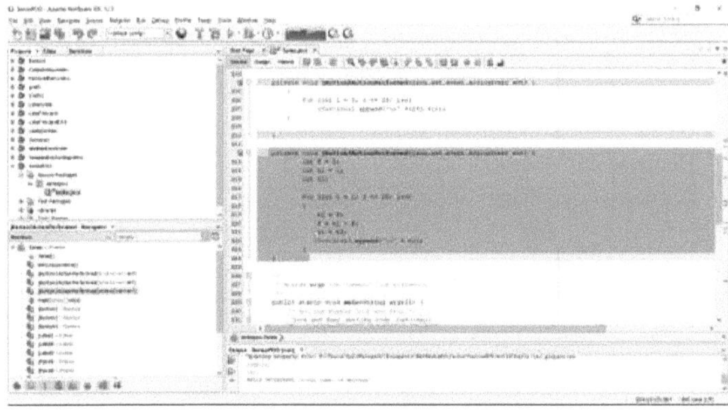

Click on compile and then on run

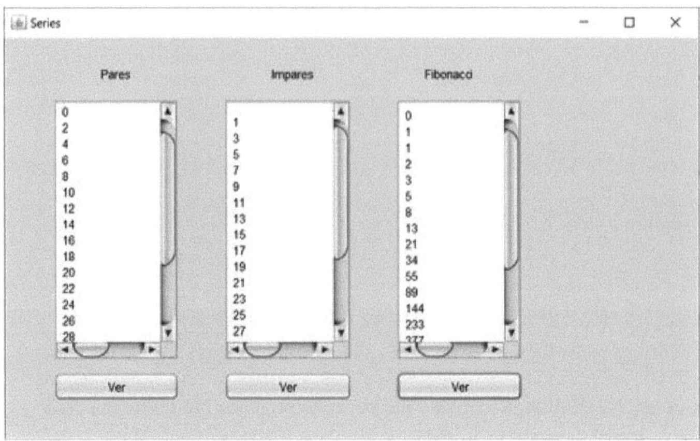

For cousins:

We select from the palette, a jPanel and in the jPanel we place a jLabel, a jButton, a jTextArea and we do the same process as above:

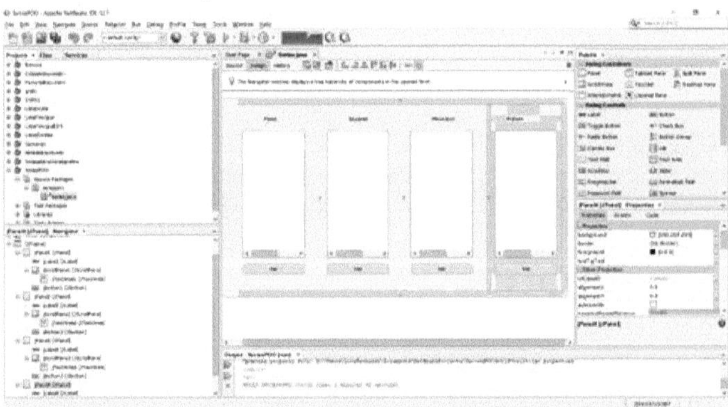

Double click on the JButton, to activate the click event, place the following code

```
private void jButton4ActionPerformed(java.awt.event.ActionEvent evt) {
int counter = 0, num = 1, auxiliary = 0;
do
{
for (int i = 1; i <= num; i++)
if (num % i == 0)
counter = counter + 1;
if (counter <= 2)
{
jTextArea4.append("\n" + num);
auxiliary++;
}
num++;
counter = 0;
```

```
} while (auxiliary <= 20);
}
```

Having:

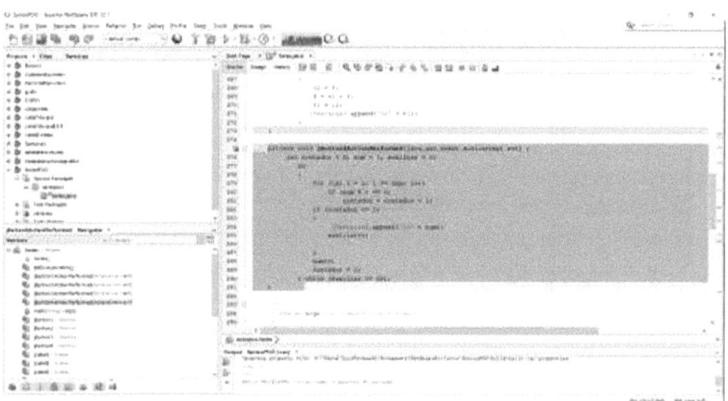

Click on compile and then on run

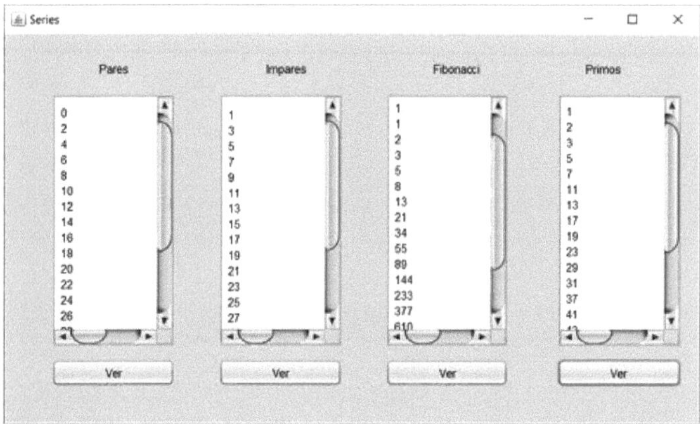

6. BIBLIOGRAPHY:

- Deitel, P., & Deitel, H. (2017). Java: How to Program (10th ed.). Pearson.
- Eckel, B. (2017). Thinking in Java (4th ed.). Prentice Hall.
- Flanagan, D. (2018). Java in a Nutshell: A Desktop Quick Reference (7th ed.). O'Reilly Media.
- Friesen, J. (2019). Java Programming for Beginners. Independently published.
- Gaddis, T. (2018). Starting Out with Java: Early Objects (6th ed.). Pearson.
- Horstmann, C. S. (2019). Core Java, Volume I: Fundamentals (12th ed.). Pearson.
- Liang, Y. D. (2019). Introduction to Java Programming and Data Structures (12th ed.). Pearson.
- Schilde, M. (2016). Java 8 in Action: Lambdas, Streams, and Functional-Style

Programming. Manning Publications.

- Sharan, M. (2017). NetBeans: The Definitive Guide (2nd ed.). O'Reilly Media.
- Sierra, K., & Bates, B. (2020). Head First Java (3rd ed.). O'Reilly Media.

PRACTICE 2

1. **TOPIC:** Classroom Basics
2. **OBJECTIVES:**

- Acquire the basic concepts related to OOP.
- Recognise the characteristics of the OOP

3. **SUSTAINABLE DEVELOPMENT GOALS:**

Indicator 4.7: By 2030, ensure that all learners acquire the knowledge and skills needed to promote sustainable development, including through education for sustainable development and sustainable lifestyles, human rights, gender equality, promotion of a culture of peace and non-violence, global citizenship and appreciation of cultural diversity and the contribution of culture to sustainable development

4. **INTRODUCTION:**

Java is a general-purpose, object-oriented, typed, object-oriented programming language, which allows the development of applications ranging from basic applications, through enterprise applications to mobile applications.

Java was born as a programming language that could be cross-platform and multi-device, under the "Write Once Run Anywhere" (WORA) paradigm.

In this way a Java program written once can be run on different platforms, being supported on Windows, MacOs and UNIX operating systems. And in turn on different types of devices.

In order to follow this paradigm, the compilation of a Java program does not generate source code, but generates bytecodes. These bytecodes are interpreted by a virtual machine or JVM (Java Virtual Machine). This machine is already written for each of the operating systems in question.

Java language features

Among the features of the Java language we find:

Platform Independent

When compiling Java source code, no specific machine code is generated, but bytecodes are generated, which are interpreted by the Java Virtual Machine (JVM), making it possible for the same source code to be executed on multiple platforms.

Object Oriented

Any element of the Java language is an object. Within objects, data is encapsulated, which is accessed by mëtodos.

Simple

Java is intended to be an easy language to learn. You simply need to understand the basic concepts of object-oriented programming (OOP).

Insurance

It is secure because programs run inside the Java Virtual Machine (JVM) in a "sandbox" format, so they cannot access anything outside of it.
It has a validation on the bytecodes to check for illegal fragment codes.
Neutral Architecture
Regardless of whether it runs on 32bit or 64bit architecture. In Java, data types always take up the same amount of space.
Portable
Java has no platform dependencies, which makes it portable to different platforms.
Robust
The Java language attempts to control error situations in the compilation and execution processes, thus reducing the risk of failure.
In addition, Java takes full control of memory by allocating and removing it through a garbage collector, so that we cannot use pointers to access it.
Multi-thread
Java allows concurrent programming, so that a single program can open different threads.
Interpreted
The bytecodes are interpreted in real time to machine code.
High Performance
Java offers Just-In-Time compilers that allow for high performance.
Distributed
The Java language is intended to run on distributed architectures, such as the Internet.

5. DEVELOPMENT:

"Netbeans login

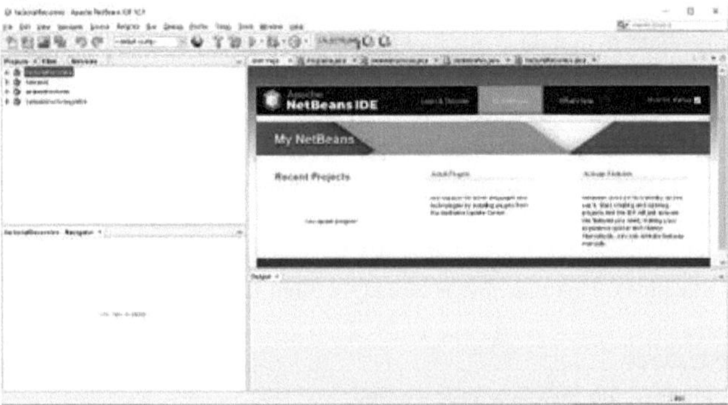

"We created a new project:

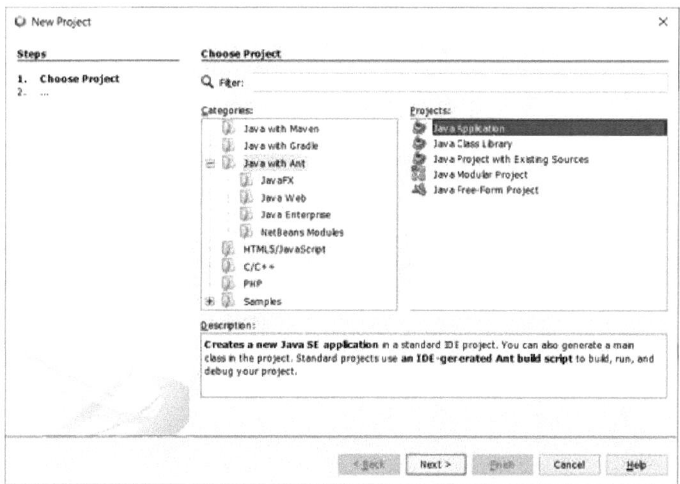

"We place as name

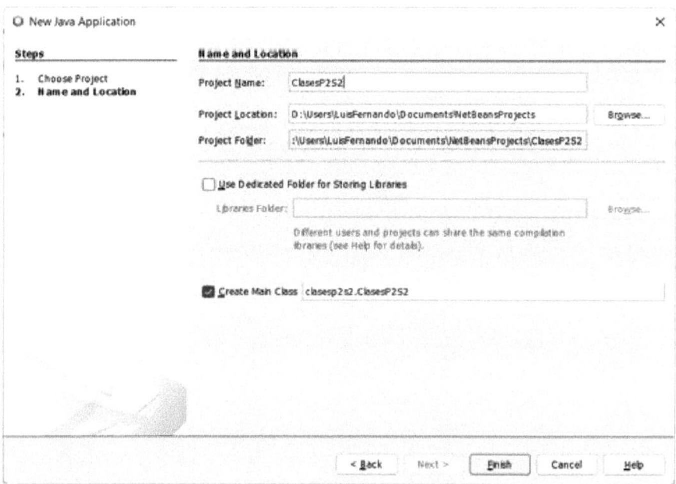

Click on finalizer

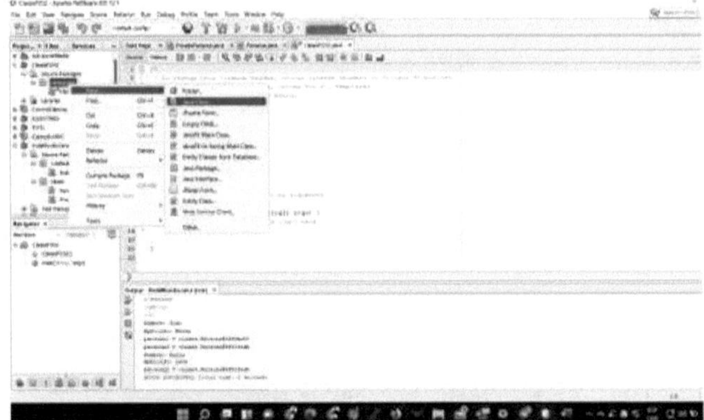

Right click on the package and add:

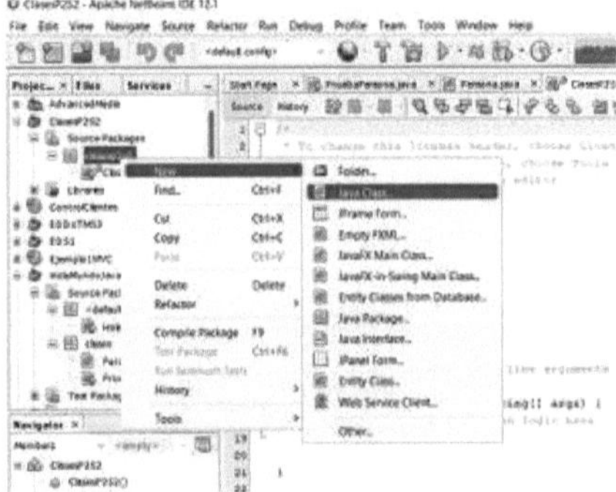

Enter the following name and then click on finalizer

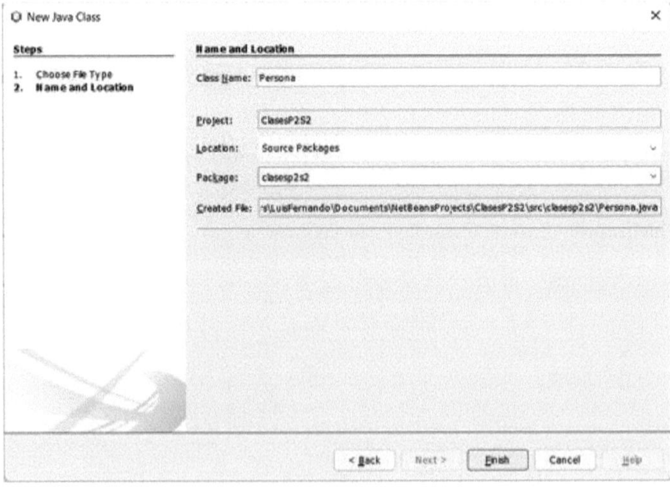

Having:

In the classroom we place the following:

```
public class Person { //Attributes of the String class name;
String surname;
//Methods of the class
public void deployInformation(){
System.out.println("Name: " + name);
System.out.println("Last name: " + last name); }
```

Having:

We select the attributes:

Having:

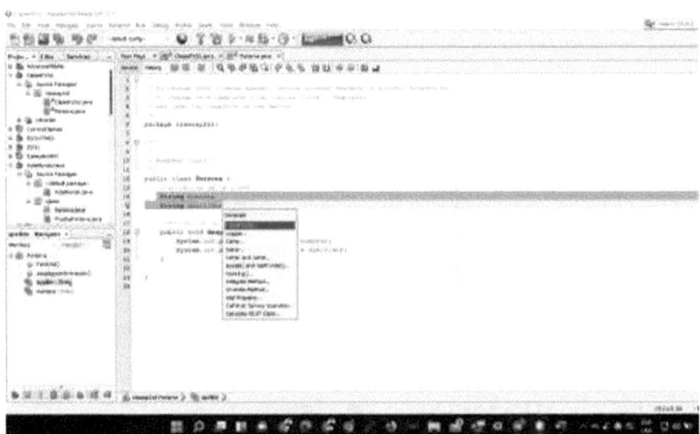

And we give in generate

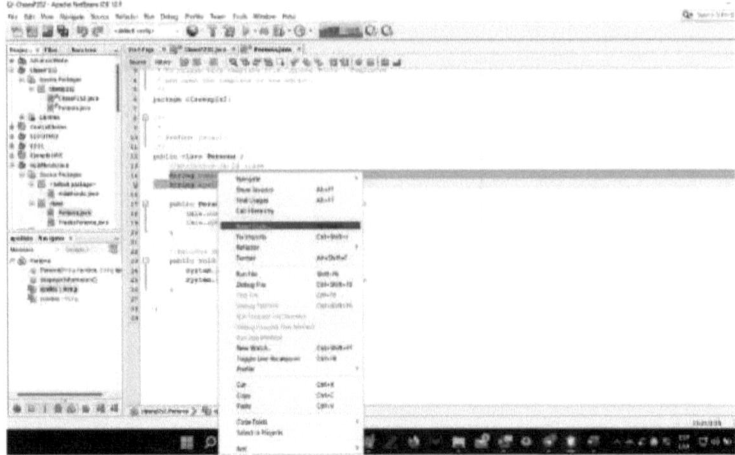

Having:

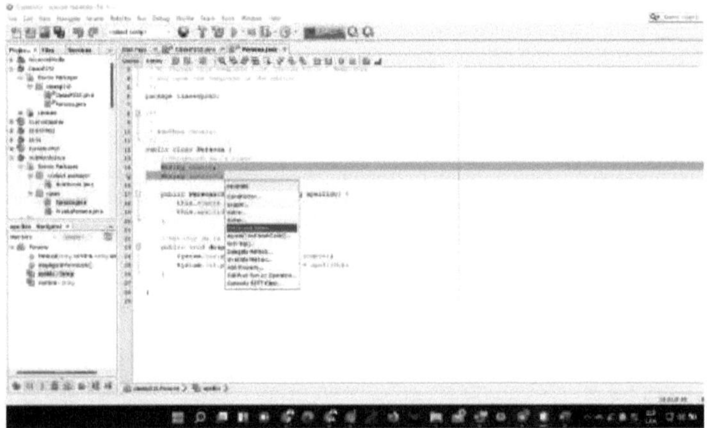

Having:

We hit generate:

In the classroom

We place the following:

```
public class ClassesP2S2 {
/**
* @param args the command line arguments
*/
```

```
public static void main(String[] args) { Person person person1 = new Persona();
person1.name = "John";
person1.surname = "Perez";
person1.displayInformation();
Person person2 = new Person();
System.out.println("person1 = " + person1);
System.out.println("person2 = " + person2);
person2.name = "Karla";
person2.surname = "Lara";
person2.displayInformation();
System.out.println("person2 = " + person2);
}
}
```

Having:

We include an empty constructor in Persona public Persona() {
}

Having:

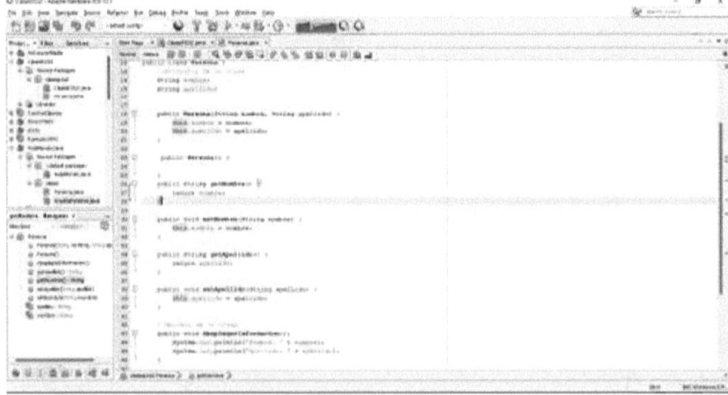

Compile and Execute:

6. BIBLIOGRAPHY:

- Deitel, P., & Deitel, H. (2017). Java: How to Program (10th ed.). Pearson.
- Eckel, B. (2017). Thinking in Java (4th ed.). Prentice Hall.
- Flanagan, D. (2018). Java in a Nutshell: A Desktop Quick Reference (7th ed.). O'Reilly Media.
- Friesen, J. (2019). Java Programming for Beginners. Independently published.
- Gaddis, T. (2018). Starting Out with Java: Early Objects (6th ed.). Pearson.
- Horstmann, C. S. (2019). Core Java, Volume I: Fundamentals (12th ed.). Pearson.
- Liang, Y. D. (2019). Introduction to Java Programming and Data Structures (12th ed.). Pearson.
- Schilde, M. (2016). Java 8 in Action: Lambdas, Streams, and Functional-Style Programming. Manning Publications.
- Sharan, M. (2017). NetBeans: The Definitive Guide (2nd ed.). O'Reilly Media.
- Sierra, K., & Bates, B. (2020). Head First Java (3rd ed.). O'Reilly Media.

PRACTICE 3

1. **TOPIC:** Inheritance in Java
2. **OBJECTIVES:**

- Acquire the basic concepts related to OOP.
- Recognise the characteristics of the OOP

3. **SUSTAINABLE DEVELOPMENT GOALS:**

Indicator 4.7: By 2030, ensure that all learners acquire the knowledge and skills needed to promote sustainable development, including through education for sustainable development and sustainable lifestyles, human rights, gender equality, promotion of a culture of peace and non-violence, global citizenship and appreciation of cultural diversity and the contribution of culture to sustainable development

4. **INTRODUCTION:**

Inheritance is an important pillar of OOP (Object Oriented Programming). It is the mechanism in Java by which a class can inherit the features (attributes and methods) of another class. Learn more below.

In the Java language, an inheriting class is called a superclass. The inheriting class is called a subclass. Thus, a subclass is a specialised version of a superclass. It inherits all the variables and methods defined by the superclass and adds its own unique elements.

Important terminology

Superclass: the class whose characteristics are inherited is known as a superclass (or a base class or a main class).

Subclass: the class that inherits the other class is known as a subclass (or a derived class, extended class or child class). The subclass can add its own fields and methods in addition to the fields and methods of the superclass.

Reuse: Inheritance supports the concept of "reuse", i.e. when we want to create a new class and there is already a class that includes some of the code we want, we can derive our new class from the existing class. By doing this, we are reusing the fields/attributes and methods of the existing class.

5. DEVELOPMENT:

- Log in to Netbeans

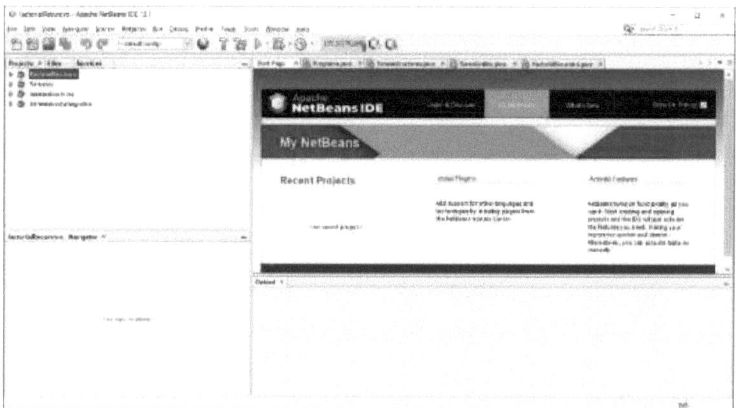

- We create a new project:

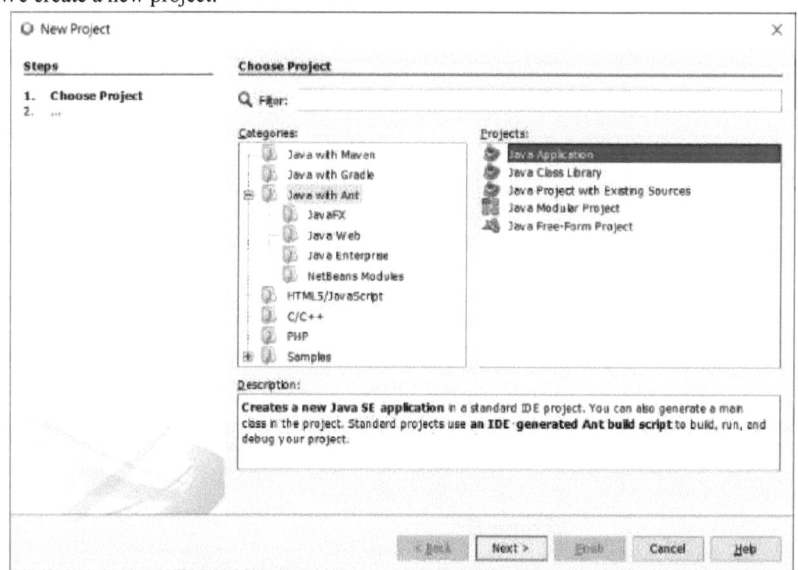

We place as name

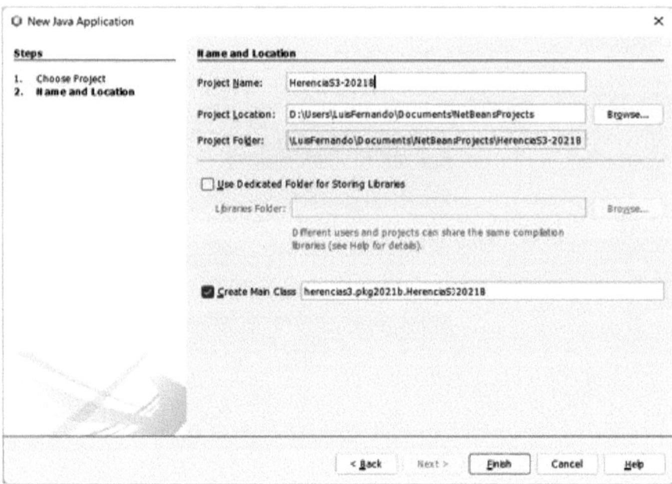

Click on finalizer

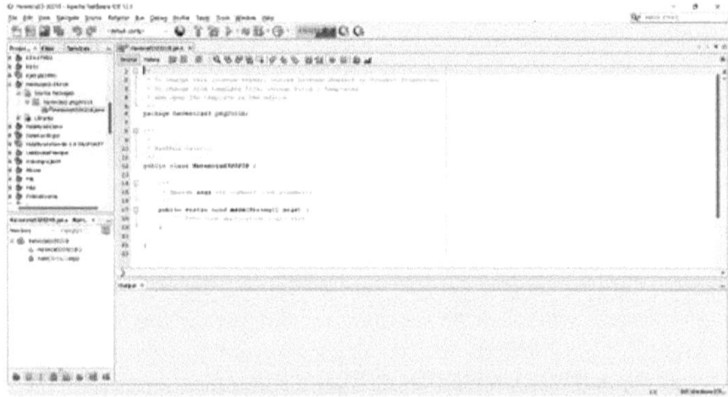

Right click on the package and add a new class with the name:

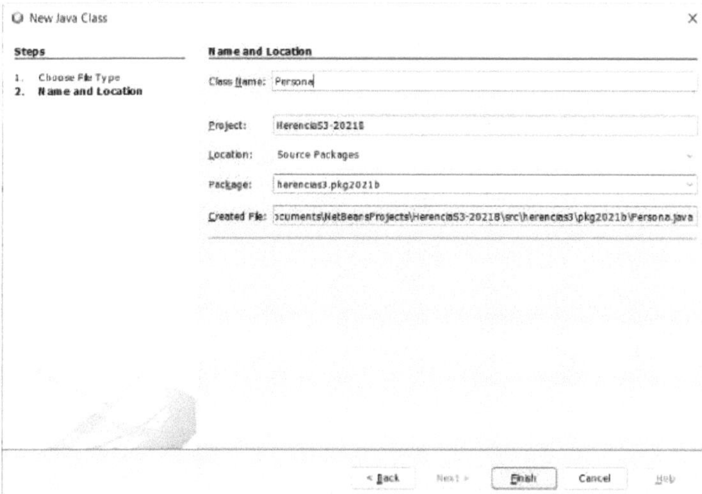

Enter the following name and then click on finalise

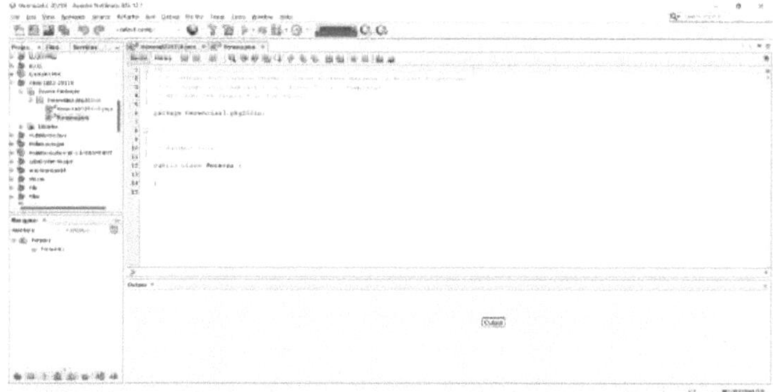

In the classroom we place the following:

```
public class Person{
protected String name;
protected char genero;
protected int age;
protected String address;
public Persona(){
}
public Persona(String name){ this.name = name;
}
public Persona(String name, char gender, int age, String address) { this.name = name;
this.gender = gender;
this.age = age;
this.address = address;
```

```
}
public String getDireccion() { return this.direccion;
}
public void setAddress(String address) { this.address = address;
}
public String getName() { return this.name;
}
public void setName(String name) { this.name = name;
}
public char getGenero() { return this.genero;
}
public void setGenero(char genero) { this.genero = genero;
}
public int getEld() { return this.age;
}
public void setEdad(int age) { this.age = age;
}
@Override
public String toString() {
StringBuilder sb = new StringBuilder();
sb.append("Person{name=").append(name);
sb.append(", gender=").append(gender);
sb.append(", age=").append(age);
sb.append(", address=").append(address);
sb.append(", ").append(super.toString());
sb.append('}');
return sb.toString();
}
}
```

Having:

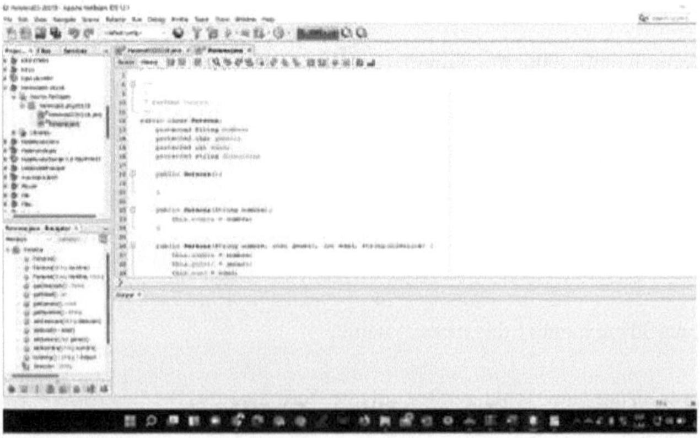

Right click on the package and add a new class with the name:

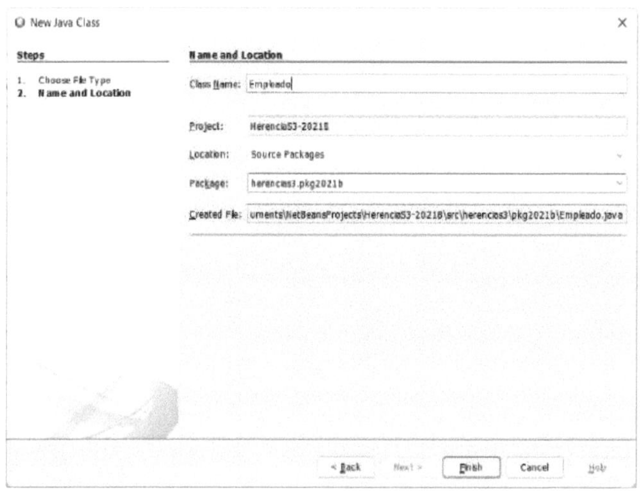

We place the following code:

```
public class Employee extends Person{
private int idEmployee;
private double sueldo;
private static static int counterEmployee;
public Employee(String name, double salary) { super(name);
this.idEmployee = ++Employee.counterEmployee; this.salary = salary;
}
public int getIdEmployee() {
return this.idEmployee;
}
public double getSalary() { return salary;
}
public void setSueldo(double sueldo) { this.sueldo = sueldo;
}
@Override
public String toString() {
StringBuilder sb = new StringBuilder();
sb.append("Employee{idEmployee=").append(this.idEmployee);
sb.append(", salary=").append(this.salary);
sb.append(", ").append(super.toString());
sb.append('}');
return sb.toString();
}
}
```

Having:

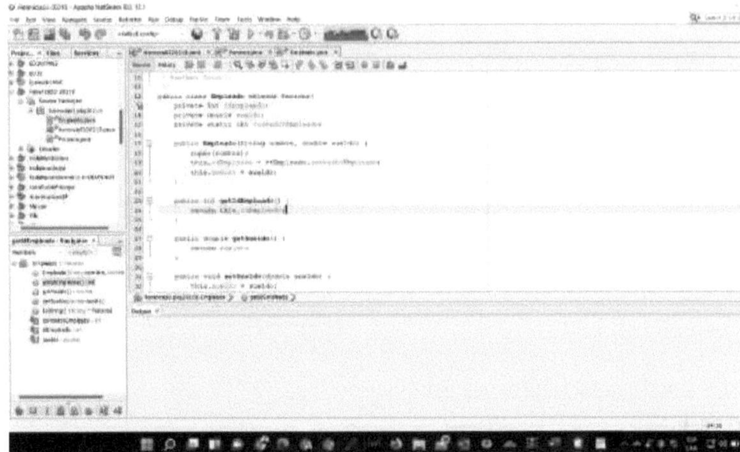

Right click on the package and add a new class with the name Client.
We place this code

```
import java.util.Date;
public class Customer extends Person{
private int idClient;
private Date date dateRecord;
private boolean vip;
private static static int counterClient;
public Cliente(Date fechaRegistro, boolean vip, String nombre, char género, int edad, String direccion){
super(name, gender, age, address);
this.idClient = ++Client.counterClient;
this.dateRecord = dateRecord;
this.vip = vip;
}
public int getIdClient() { return idClient;
}
public Date getDateRecord() {
return dateRecord;
}
public void setDateRecord(Date dateRecord) { this.dateRecord = dateRecord;
}
public boolean isVip() { return vip;
}
public void setVip(boolean vip) { this.vip = vip;
}
@Override
public String toString() {
StringBuilder sb = new StringBuilder();
sb.append("Customer{idClient=").append(idClient);
```

```
sb.append(", dateRecord=").append(dateRecord);
sb.append(", vip=").append(vip);
sb.append(", ").append(super.toString());
sb.append('}');
return sb.toString();
}
}
```

Having:

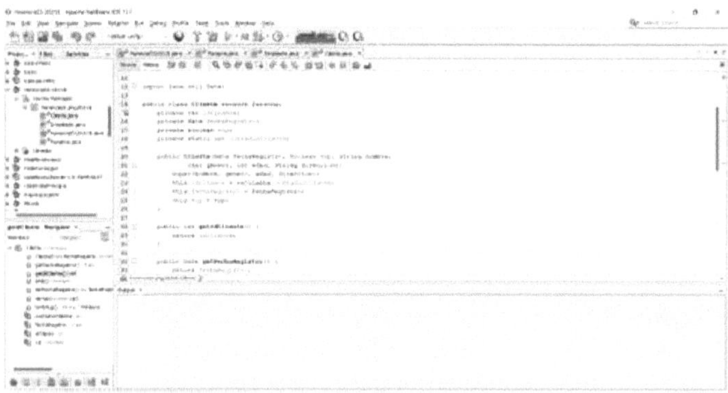

We select the class:

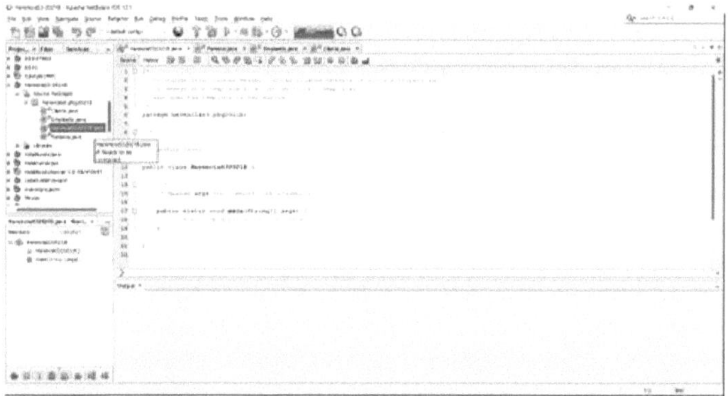

We place the following code:

```
import java.util.*;
public class InheritanceS32021B {
/**
* @param args the command line arguments
*/
public static void main(String[] args) { // TODO code application logic here Employee
employee1 = new Employee("John", 5000.0); System.out.println("employee1 = " +
employee1);
```

Customer customer1 = new Customer(new Date(), true, "Karla", 'F', 28, "Saturn 15")
System.out.println("customer1 = " + customer1);
Having:

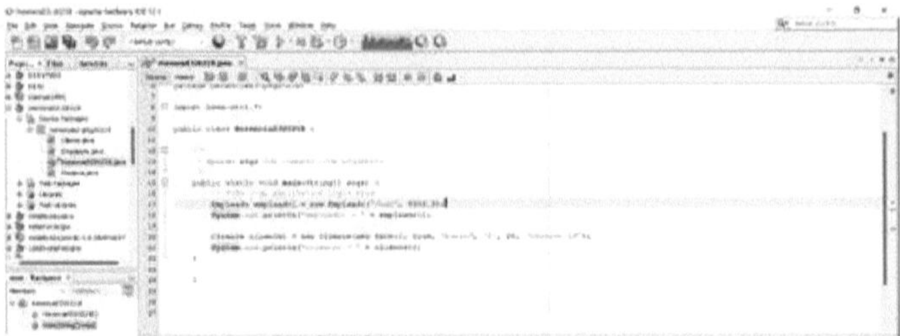

Compile and run:

6. BIBLIOGRAPHY:

- Deitel, P., & Deitel, H. (2017). Java: How to Program (10th ed.). Pearson.
- Eckel, B. (2017). Thinking in Java (4th ed.). Prentice Hall.
- Flanagan, D. (2018). Java in a Nutshell: A Desktop Quick Reference (7th ed.). O'Reilly Media.
- Friesen, J. (2019). Java Programming for Beginners. Independently published.
- Gaddis, T. (2018). Starting Out with Java: Early Objects (6th ed.). Pearson.
- Horstmann, C. S. (2019). Core Java, Volume I: Fundamentals (12th ed.). Pearson.
- Liang, Y. D. (2019). Introduction to Java Programming and Data Structures (12th ed.). Pearson.
- Schilde, M. (2016). Java 8 in Action: Lambdas, Streams, and Functional-Style Programming. Manning Publications.
- Sharan, M. (2017). NetBeans: The Definitive Guide (2nd ed.). O'Reilly Media.
- Sierra, K., & Bates, B. (2020). Head First Java (3rd ed.). O'Reilly Media.

PRACTICE 4

1. **TOPIC:** Generic Classes in Java
2. **OBJECTIVES:**

- Acquire the basic concepts related to Java.
- Recognise the features of Java

3. **SUSTAINABLE DEVELOPMENT GOALS:**

Indicator 4.7: By 2030, ensure that all learners acquire the knowledge and skills needed to promote sustainable development, including through education for sustainable development and sustainable lifestyles, human rights, gender equality, promotion of a culture of peace and non-violence, global citizenship and appreciation of cultural diversity and the contribution of culture to sustainable development

4. **INTRODUCTION:**

The term generic means **parameterised types**. Parameterised types are important because they allow you to **create classes, interfaces and methods in which the type of data on which they operate is specified as a parameter**. A class, interface or method that operates on a parameterised type is called generic, such as a **generic class** or **generic method**.
A major advantage of generic code is that it will automatically work with the data type passed to its type parameter. Many algorithms are logically the same, regardless of the type of data to which they apply. For example, a Quicksort (sorting algorithm) is the same whether you are sorting Integer, String, Object, or Thread elements. With generics, you can define an algorithm once, regardless of any specific data type, and then apply that algorithm to a wide variety of data types without any additional effort.
It is important to understand that Java has always given you the ability to create classes, interfaces and generalised methods by operating on references of the type **Object**. Because *Object* is the superclass of all other classes, an *Object* reference can refer to any type of object. Thus, in pre-genre code, classes, interfaces and generalised methods used references to objects to operate on various data types.
The problem was that they could not do this with type safety because conversions were needed to convert expbcitly from Object to the actual type of data being operated on. Therefore, it was possible to accidentally create type mismatches. Genbrics add the missing type safety because they make these conversions automatic and seamless. In short, genbrics enhance your ability to reuse code and allow you to do so safely and reliably.

5. **DEVELOPMENT:**

- Log in to Netbeans

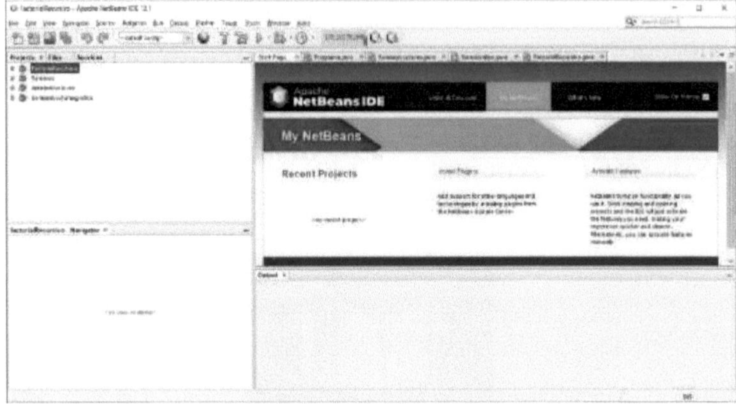

- We create a new project:

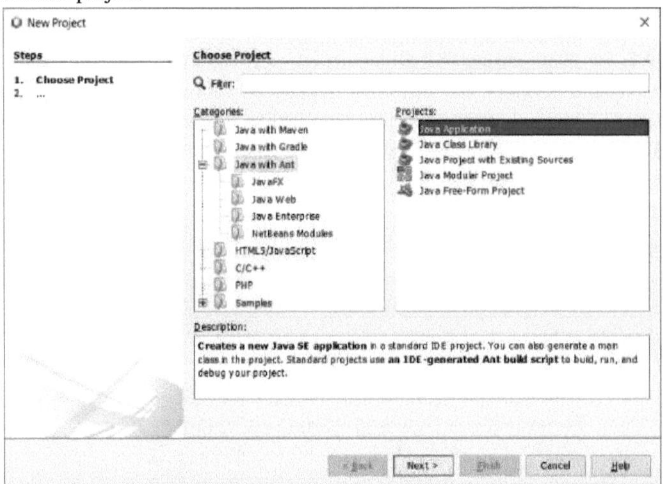

- We place as name

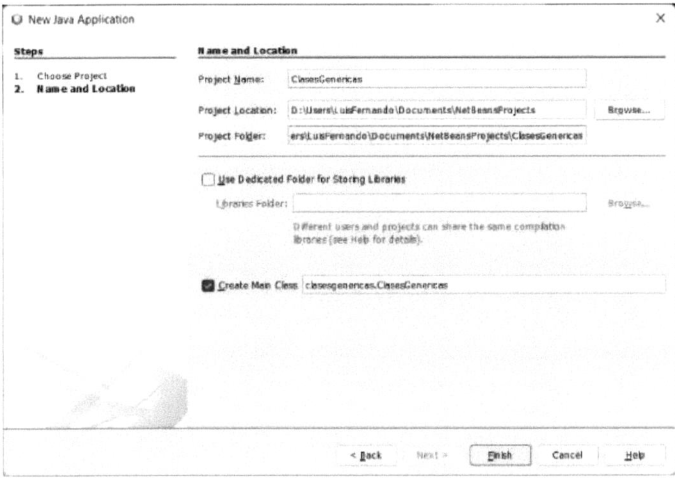

Having:

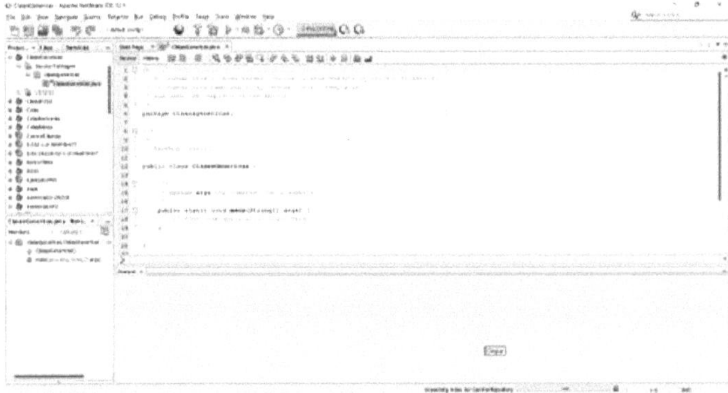

We create a new class

With the name:

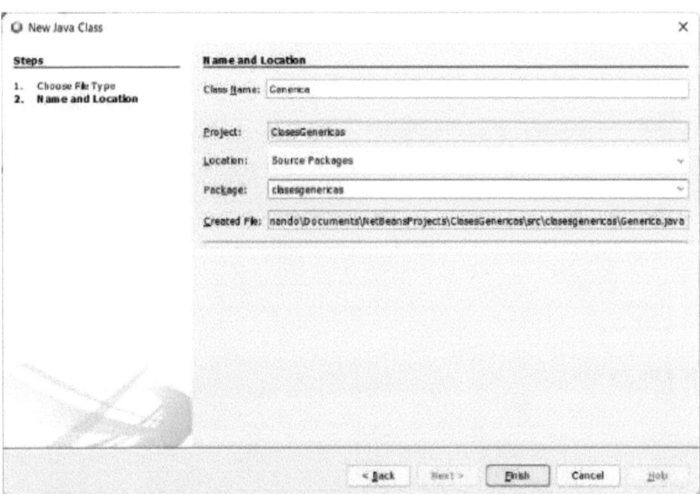

We place the following code:

```
public class Generica <T> {
private T object;
public Generica(T object){ this.object = object;
}
public void getType(){
System.out.println("Type T is: " + object.getClass().getSimpleName());
}
}
```

Having:

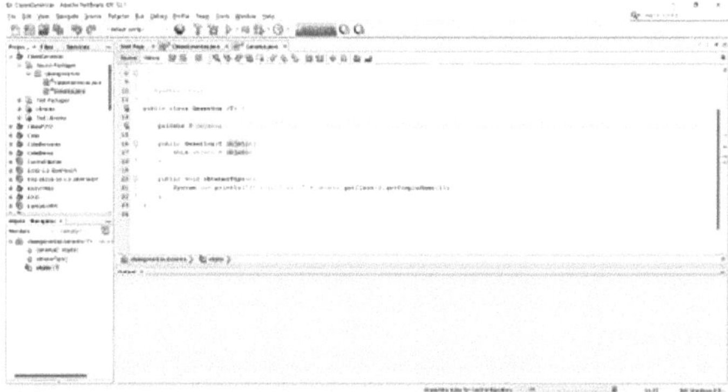

In the classroom:

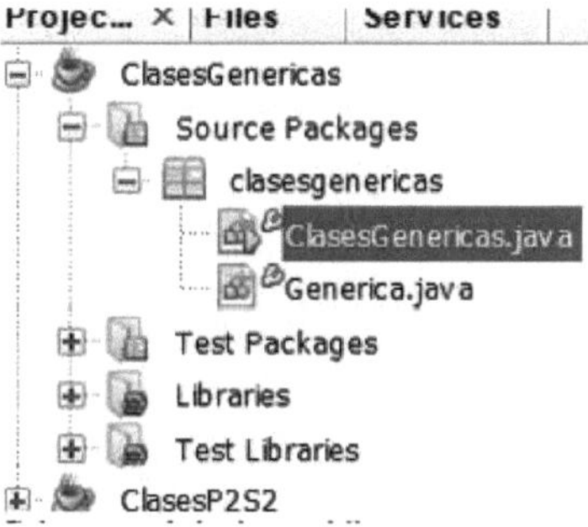

We place the following code: public class GenericaGenericas { public static void main(String[] args) { Generica<Integer> objectInt = new Generica(15); objectInt.getType(); Generica<String> objectString = new Generica("John"); objectString.getType(); }
}

Having:

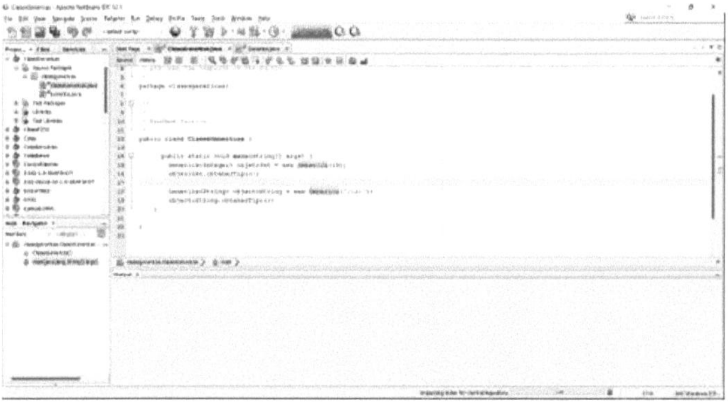

Compile and Execute:

6. BIBLIOGRAPHY:

- Deitel, P., & Deitel, H. (2017). Java: How to Program (10th ed.). Pearson.
- Eckel, B. (2017). Thinking in Java (4th ed.). Prentice Hall.
- Flanagan, D. (2018). Java in a Nutshell: A Desktop Quick Reference (7th ed.). O'Reilly Media.
- Friesen, J. (2019). Java Programming for Beginners. Independently published.
- Gaddis, T. (2018). Starting Out with Java: Early Objects (6th ed.). Pearson.
- Horstmann, C. S. (2019). Core Java, Volume I: Fundamentals (12th ed.). Pearson.
- Liang, Y. D. (2019). Introduction to Java Programming and Data Structures (12th ed.). Pearson.
- Schilde, M. (2016). Java 8 in Action: Lambdas, Streams, and Functional-Style Programming. Manning Publications.
- Sharan, M. (2017). NetBeans: The Definitive Guide (2nd ed.). O'Reilly Media.
- Sierra, K., & Bates, B. (2020). Head First Java (3rd ed.). O'Reilly Media.

PRACTICE 5

1. **TOPIC:** Files in Java
2. **OBJECTIVES:**

- Acquire the basic concepts related to Java.
- Recognise the features of Java

3. **SUSTAINABLE DEVELOPMENT GOALS:**

Indicator 4.7: By 2030, ensure that all learners acquire the knowledge and skills needed to promote sustainable development, including through education for sustainable development and sustainable lifestyles, human rights, gender equality, promotion of a culture of peace and non-violence, global citizenship and appreciation of cultural diversity and the contribution of culture to sustainable development

4. **INTRODUCTION:**

File Class

The File class is used to **obtain information** about files and directories.

In addition, the File class allows you to create and delete files and directories.

An object of the Java File class **represents** a file or directory.

BUILDERS

The class provides the following constructors to create File objects: public File(String filename|path);

public File(String path, String filename|path);

public File(File path, String filename|path);

The **path** can be absolute or relative.

Examples using the first constructor:

1. Creates a File Object associated with the file people.dat in the working directory:

File f = new File("personas.dat");

In this case no path is given. It is assumed that the file is in the current working directory.

2. Creates a File Object associated with the file people.dat located in the files directory within the current directory.

File f = new File("files/personas.dat");

In this case the relative path is given based on the current working directory. It is assumed that the file people.dat is located in the directory files. In turn, the directory files is located inside the current working directory.

3. Create a File Object associated to the file people.dat giving the absolute path:

File f = new File("c:/files/persons.dat");

The file is located in the directory files. In turn, the files directory is located on the root of the C drive:

If the drive letter is omitted, the drive letter of the drive where the project is located is assumed by default:

```
File f = new File("/files/personas.dat");
```

Examples using the second constructor:

In this case a File object is created whose path (absolute or relative) is indicated in the first String.

1. Creates a File Object associated with the file people.dat located in the files directory within the current directory.

```
File f = new File("files", "people.dat" );
```

In this case the relative path is given based on the current working directory.

2. Create a File Object associated to the people.dat file giving the absolute path:

```
File f = new File("/files", "people.dat" );
```

In this case the absolute path, indicated by the slash at the beginning, is indicated.

Examples using the third constructor:

This constructor allows the creation of a File object whose path is specified through another File object.

1. Create a File Object associated with the file people.dat located in the files directory within the current directory.

```
File path = new File("files");
File f = new File(path, "people.dat" );
```

2. Create a File Object associated to the people.dat file giving the absolute path:

```
File path = new File("/files");
File f = new File(path, "people.dat" );
```

Note that creating a File object does not mean that the file or directory must exist or that the path is correct.

If they do not exist, no exception will be triggered and no exception will be created.

5. DEVELOPMENT:

- Log in to Netbeans

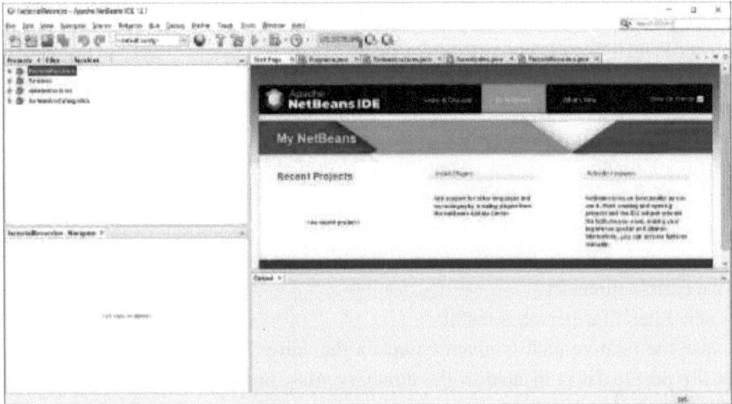

- We create a new project:

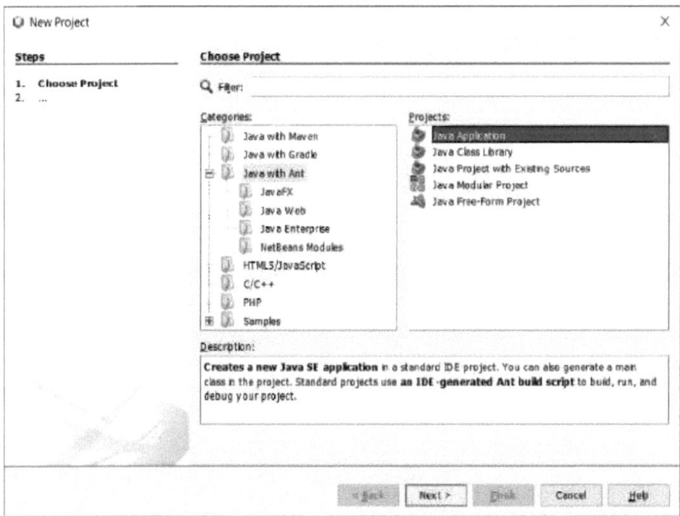

- We place as name

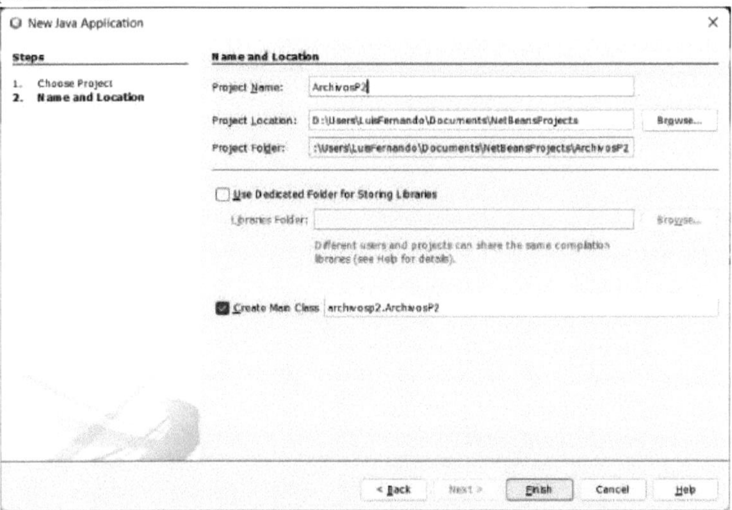

Having:

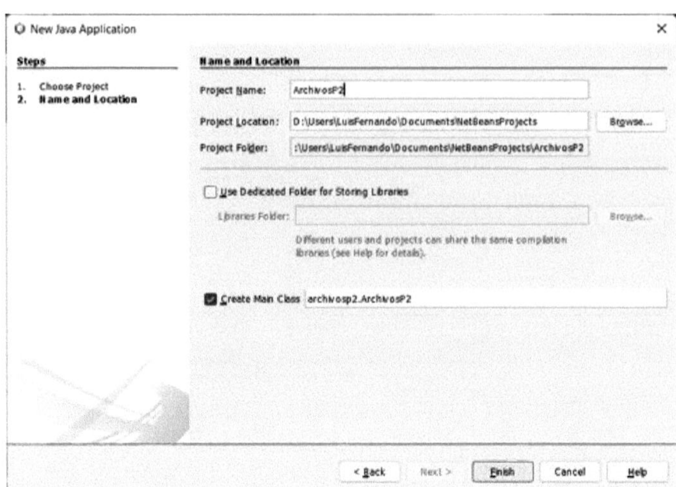

Having:

```
package archivosp2;

public class ArchivosP2 {

    public static void main(String[] args) {
    }

}
```

We eliminate:

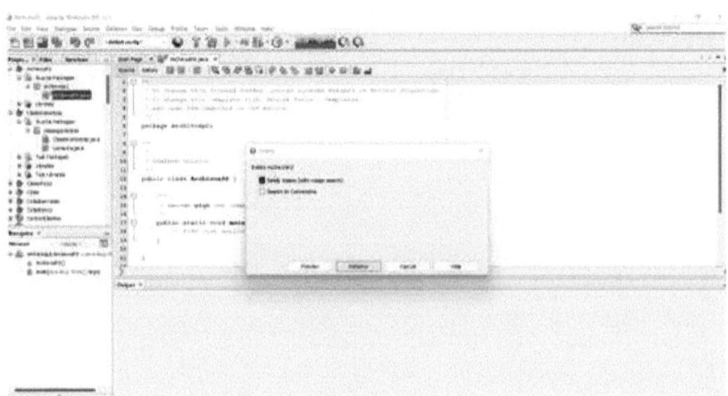

Click on refactor

We create a new JFrame

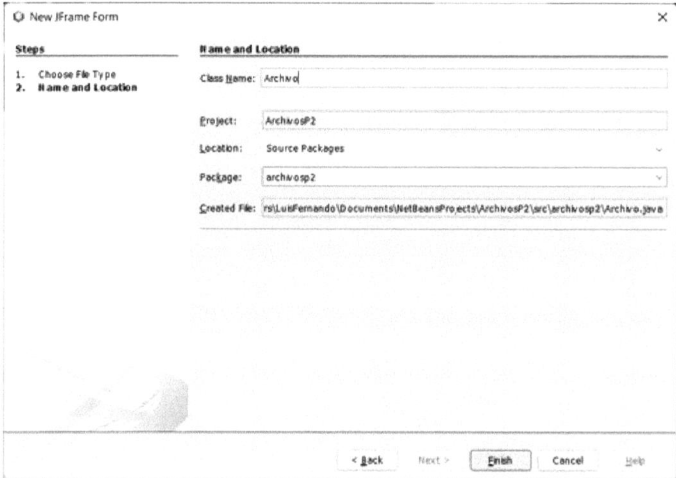

Having:

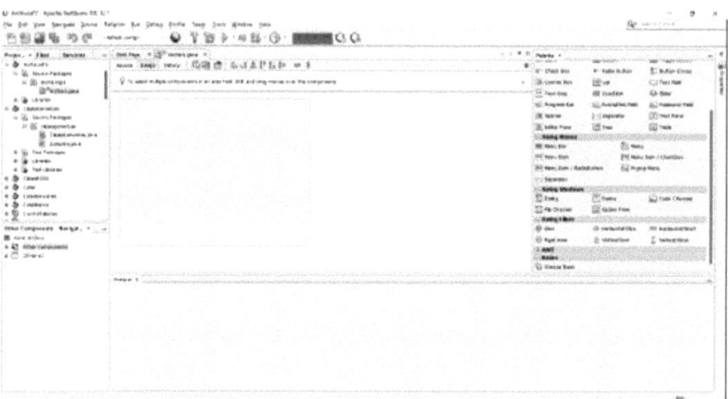

Select a menu bar

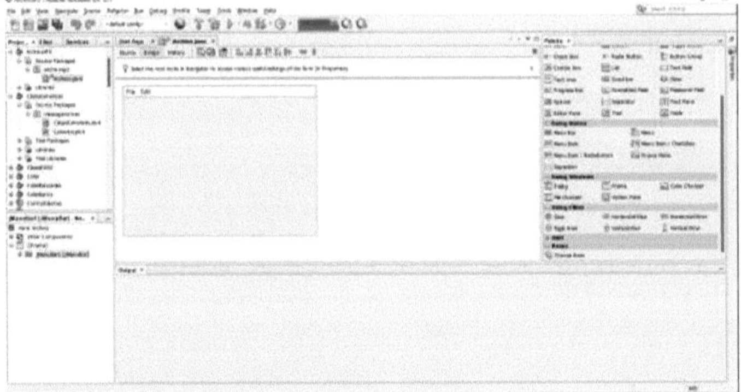

Then we insert a menu item in the menu bar.

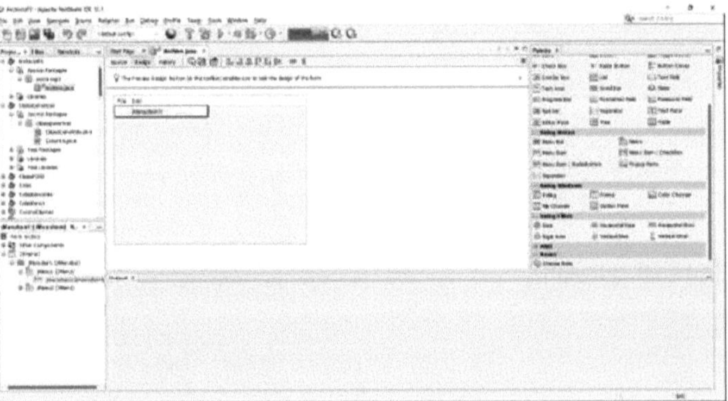

We edit

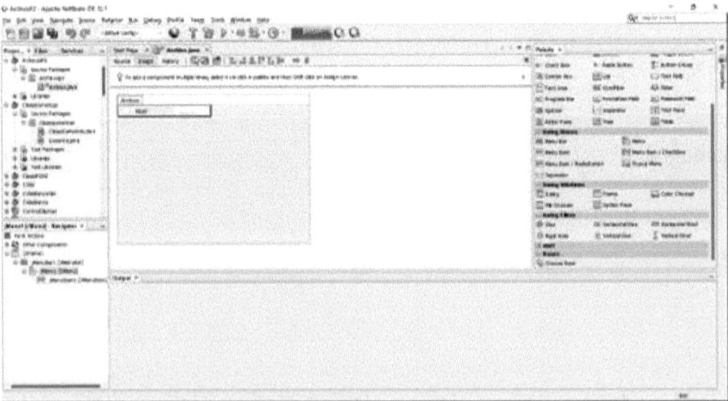

We place a TextArea

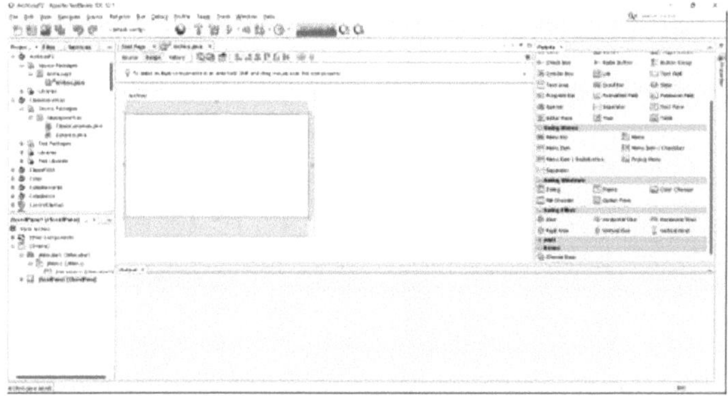

We declare the following variables and place the following imports

```
import java.io.BufferedReader;
import java.io.File;
import java.io.FileNotFoundException;
import java.io.FileReader;
import java.io.IOException;
import java.io.PrintWriter;
import java.util.logging.Level;
import java.util.logging.Logger;
import javax.swing.JFileChooser;
JFileChooser fileChooser;
int selection;
File file;
```

Having:

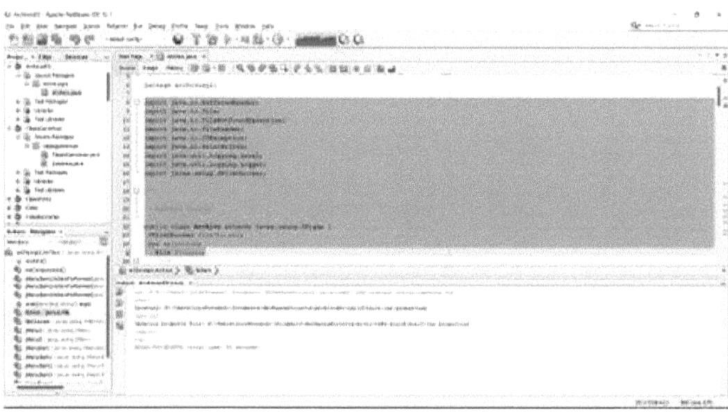

Select the next event:

We place the following code: fileChooser = new JFileChooser(); selected= fileChooser.showSaveDialog(jTextArea1); file= fileChooser.getSelectedFile(); BufferedReader reader=null; String line=""; try { reader = new BufferedReader(new FileReader(file)); } catch (FileNotFoundException ex) {
Logger.getLogger(File.class.getName()).log(Level.SEVERE, null, ex); }
try { line = reader.readLine(); } catch (IOException ex) {
Logger.getLogger(File.class.getName()).log(Level.SEVERE, null, ex); }
while (line != null) {
jTextArea1.append(line); jTextArea1.append(System.getProperty("line.separator")); try { line = reader.readLine(); } catch (IOException ex) {
Logger.getLogger(File.class.getName()).log(Level.SEVERE, null, ex); }
}
Having:

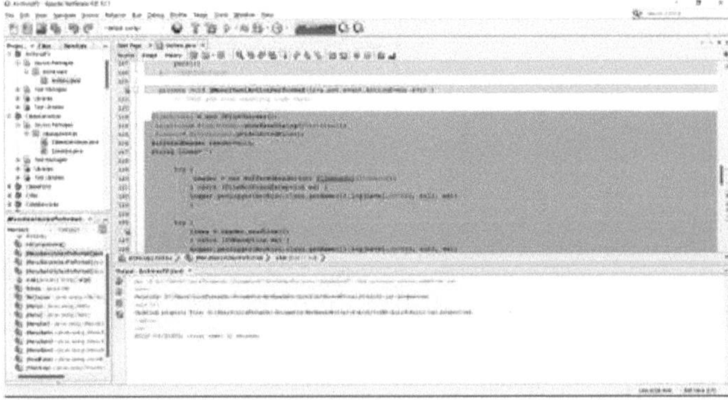

We go to the layout and place the following:

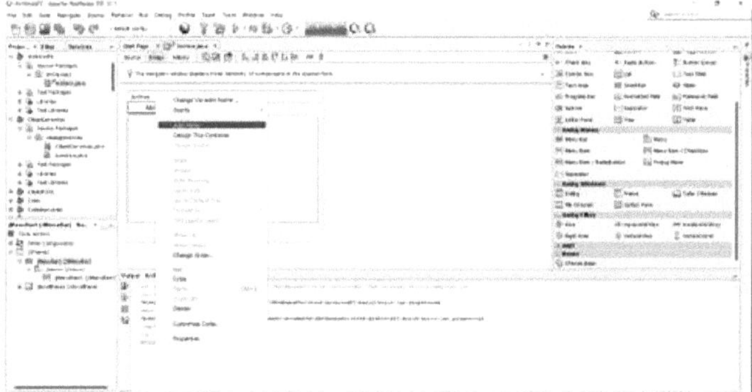

Having:

Change and put Edit and add a new menu item

At the event:

We place the following code:
jTextArea1.setText(" ");
Having:

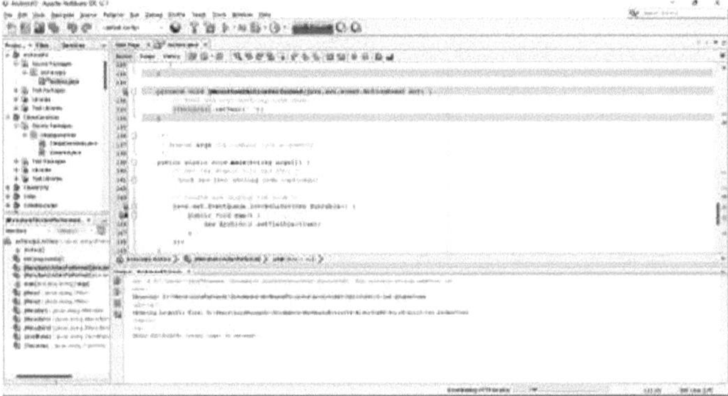

We place another Menu item, with the name of save

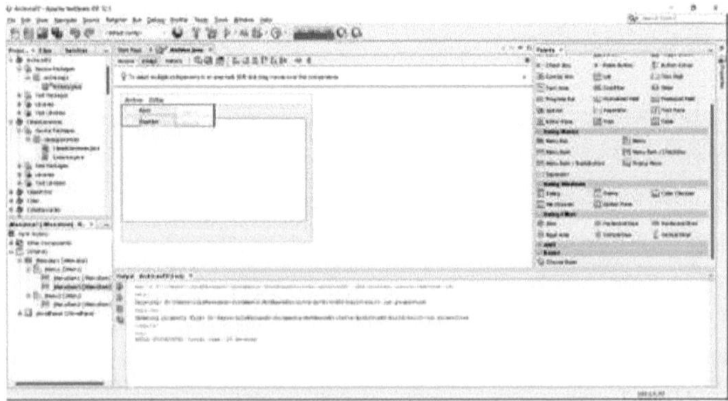

Select the event:

Compile and Execute:

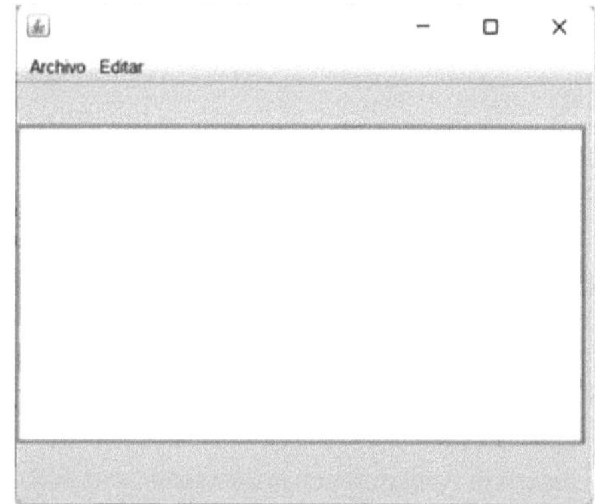

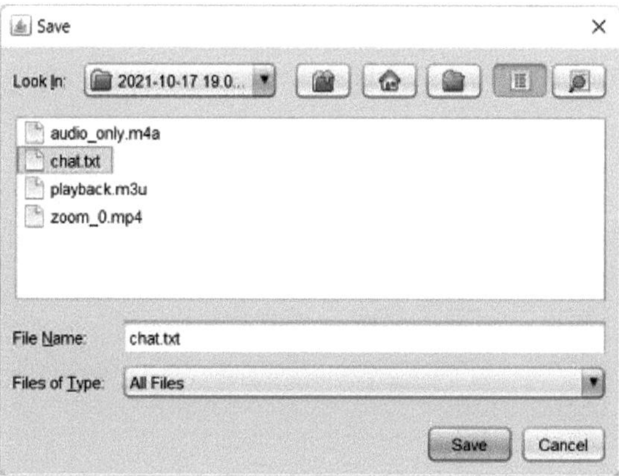

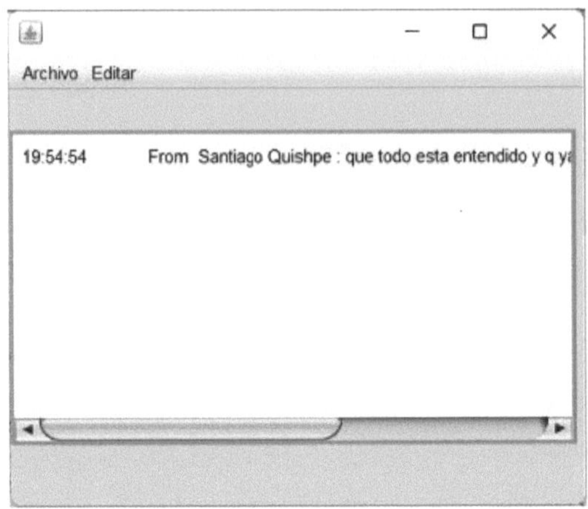

6. BIBLIOGRAPHY:

- Deitel, P., & Deitel, H. (2017). Java: How to Program (10th ed.). Pearson.
- Eckel, B. (2017). Thinking in Java (4th ed.). Prentice Hall.
- Flanagan, D. (2018). Java in a Nutshell: A Desktop Quick Reference (7th ed.). O'Reilly Media.
- Friesen, J. (2019). Java Programming for Beginners. Independently published.
- Gaddis, T. (2018). Starting Out with Java: Early Objects (6th ed.). Pearson.
- Horstmann, C. S. (2019). Core Java, Volume I: Fundamentals (12th ed.). Pearson.
- Liang, Y. D. (2019). Introduction to Java Programming and Data Structures (12th ed.). Pearson.
- Schilde, M. (2016). Java 8 in Action: Lambdas, Streams, and Functional-Style Programming. Manning Publications.
- Sharan, M. (2017). NetBeans: The Definitive Guide (2nd ed.). O'Reilly Media.
- Sierra, K., & Bates, B. (2020). Head First Java (3rd ed.). O'Reilly Media.

PRACTICE 6

1. **TOPIC:** Java Databases
2. **OBJECTIVES:**

- Acquire the basic concepts related to Java.
- Recognise the features of Java

3. **SUSTAINABLE DEVELOPMENT GOALS:**

Indicator 4.7: By 2030, ensure that all learners acquire the knowledge and skills needed to promote sustainable development, including through education for sustainable development and sustainable lifestyles, human rights, gender equality, promotion of a culture of peace and non-violence, global citizenship and appreciation of cultural diversity and the contribution of culture to sustainable development

4. **INTRODUCTION:**

A database is a series of tables containing information arranged in some structure that makes it easy to access those tables, sort them and select rows from the tables according to specific criteria. Databases generally have *indexes* associated with some of their columns, so that access is as fast as possible.

Databases are, without a doubt, the most widely used structures in computers; they are the heart of systems as complex as the census of a nation, the payroll of a company, the invoicing system of a multinational, or the means by which we are issued the ticket for our next holiday. In the case, for example, of a company's employee register, you can imagine a table with employee names and addresses, and salaries, deductions and benefits. To organise this information, you could start with a table containing the names of the employees, their addresses and telephone numbers. You could also include information regarding their salary, category, last salary increase, etc.

Could all this be placed in a single table? Almost certainly not. The salary ranges for different employees are likely to be the same, so you could optimise the table by storing only the salary type in the *employee* table and the salary ranges (in euros) in another table, indexed through the salary type. For example

Key	Nombre	Tipo de Salario
1	Pérez	2
2	García	1
3	Cabrera	2
4	López	3
5	Gómez	1

Tipo de Salario	Mínimo	Máximo
1	1100	1200
2	1200	1500
3	1500	1800

The data in the *Wage Type* column refers to the second table. You can imagine many categories for these secondary tables, like for example the province of residence and the tax retention rates, or if you have life insurance, own house, car, flat on the beach, house in the countryside, etc. Each table has a first column that serves as a key for the other columns, which already contain data. The construction of tables in databases is both an art and a science, and their structure is referred to by their *normal form*. Tables are said to be in first, second or third normal form, or in abbreviated form as 1NF, 2NF or 3NF.

- Each cell in the table must have only one value (never a set of values). **(1NF)**
- 1NF and each non-key column is completely dependent on the key column. This means that there is a one-to-one relationship between the primary key and the remaining cells in the row **(2NF)**.
- (2NF) and all non-key columns are mutually independent. This means that there are no data columns containing data calculated from the data in other columns. **(3NF)**

Currently all databases are constructed in such a way that all their tables are in the Third Normal Form (3NF); that is, the databases are made up of a fairly large number of tables, each with relatively few columns of information.

When extracting data from the tables, queries are made against it. For example, if you want to generate a table of employees and their salary ranges for some kind of special plan of the company, that table does not exist directly in the database, so it must be constructed by making a query to the database, and you would obtain a table containing the following information:

Nombre	Mínimo	Máximo
Pérez	1200	1500
García	1100	1200
Cabrera	1200	1500
López	1500	1800
Gómez	1100	1200

Or perhaps mandated by the wage increase:

Nombre	Mínimo	Máximo
García	1100	1200
Gómez	1100	1200
Pérez	1200	1500
Cabrera	1200	1500
López	1500	1800

To generate the above table, a database query would have to be made in the following form:

```
SELECT DISTINCTROW Employees.Name, WageType.Minimum, WageType.Maximum
FROM Employees INNER JOIN WageType ON Employees.WageKey =
WageType.WageKey
ORDER BY WageType.Minimum;
```

The language in which the query is written is SQL, currently supported by almost all databases worldwide. The SQL standards have been various over the years and many of the PC databases support some of these types. The **SQL-92** standard is the one that is considered to be the source of all updates. It should be noted that there are later versions of SQL, refined and extended to exploit unique features of particular databases, so you should not depart from the basic standard if you intend to make an application that can attack any type of database. At the end of the chapter, the reader can find a short review of the SQL language.

Since PCs have become a ubiquitous tool in most offices, a large number of databases have been developed to run on such platforms; from very elementary databases such as *Microsoft Works*, to quite sophisticated ones such as *Approach*, *dBase*, *Paradox*, *Access* and *Foxbase.*

Another more serious category of PC databases are those that use the PC platform as a client to access a server. These databases are *IBM DB/2*, *Microsoft SQL Server*, *Oracle*, *Sybase*, *SQLBase*, *Informix*, *XDB* and *Postgres*. All of these databases support several similar dialects of SQL, and all appear, at first glance, to be interchangeable. The reason they are not interchangeable, of course, is that each is designed with different performance characteristics, user interface and programming. Although they all support SQL and the programming is similar, each database has its own way of receiving SQL queries and its own way of returning results. This is where the next level of standardisation comes in, with **ODBC** (*Open DataBase Connectivity*).

The idea is that you can write code regardless of who owns the database you want to access, so that you can extract similar results from different types of databases without touching the program code. If some form of traceroute could be written for these databases with a similar interface, the goal would not be difficult to achieve.

Microsoft made its first attempt in 1992, with the specification they called *Object Database Connectivity*, which was supposed to be the answer to connecting to any type of database from Windows. As in all computer applications, this was not the only version, but there were several until the 1994 version, which was faster and more stable, as well as being the first of the 32-bit versions. And if that wasn't enough, ODBC started to move to platforms other than Windows, taking over not only the PC but also the workstation world. So much so^ that now almost every database manufacturer provides an ODBC *driver* to access their database.

However, ODBC is far from the panacea that you might initially think it is and that Microsoft would have you believe. Many database vendors support ODBC as an *alternative interface* to their standard, and ODBC programming is far from trivial, including all the paraphernalia of Windows programming with *handles*, pointers and options that are hard to assimilate. Finally, ODBC is not a free standard, it has been developed and is owned by Microsoft, which, given the winds blowing in this competitive world of software companies, makes its future difficult to predict.

5. DEVELOPMENT:

- Log in to Netbeans

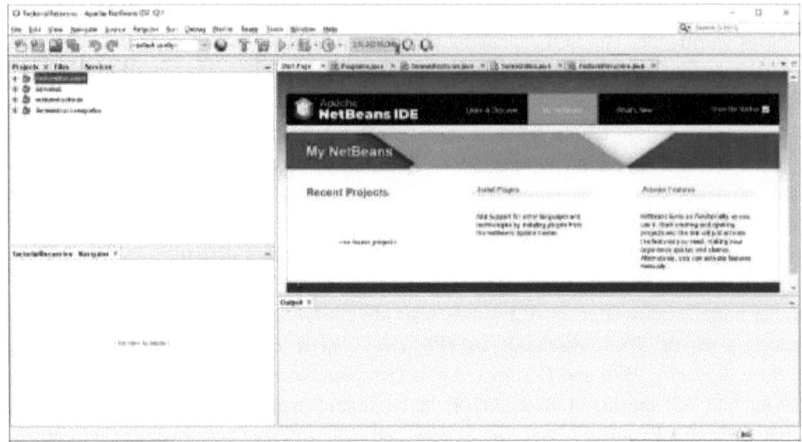

- We create a new project:

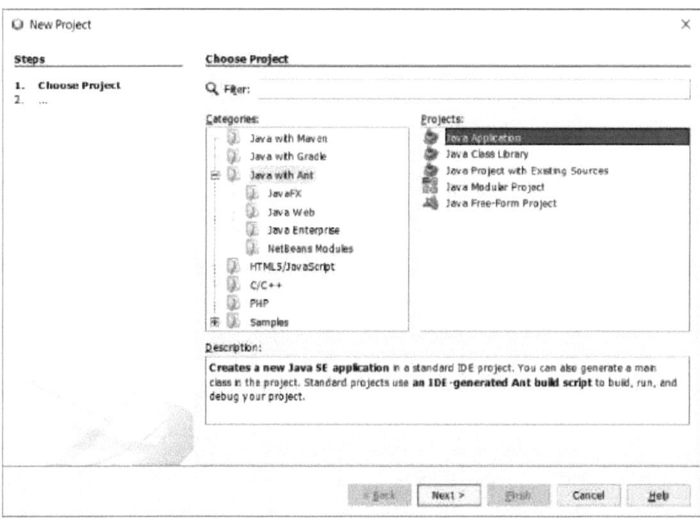

- We place as name:

Having:

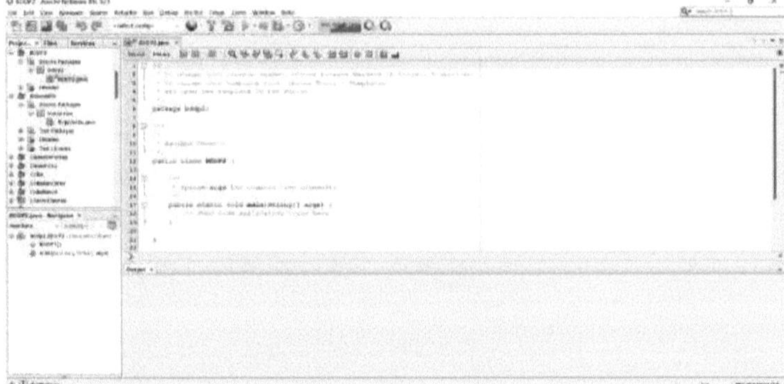

We remove the class

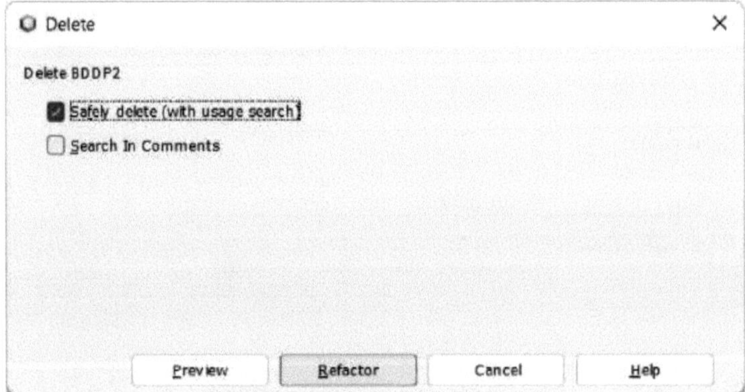

We create a JFrame:

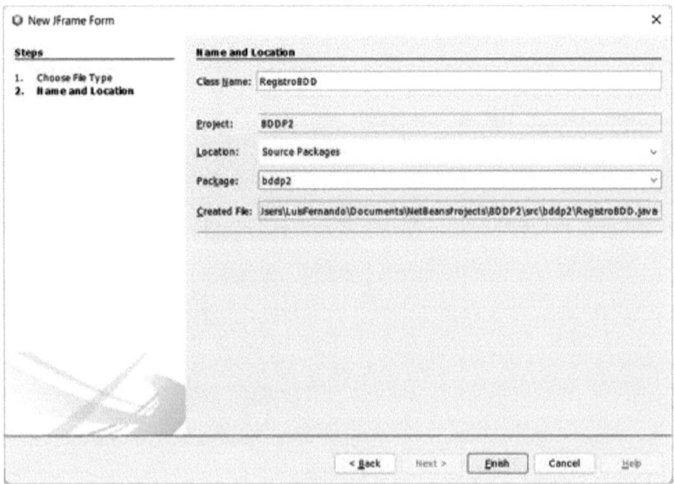

We create the following structure:

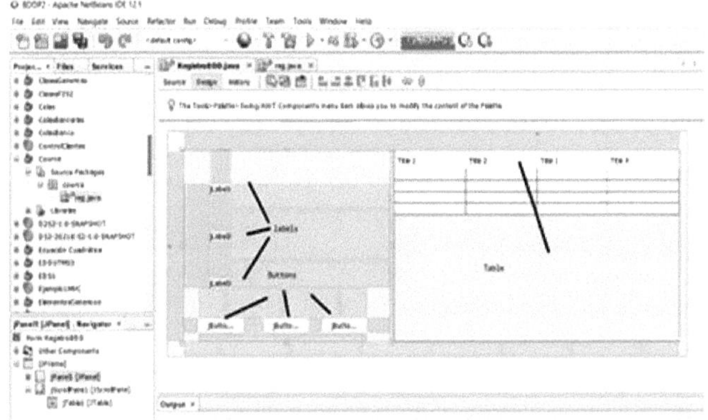

We place the following names:

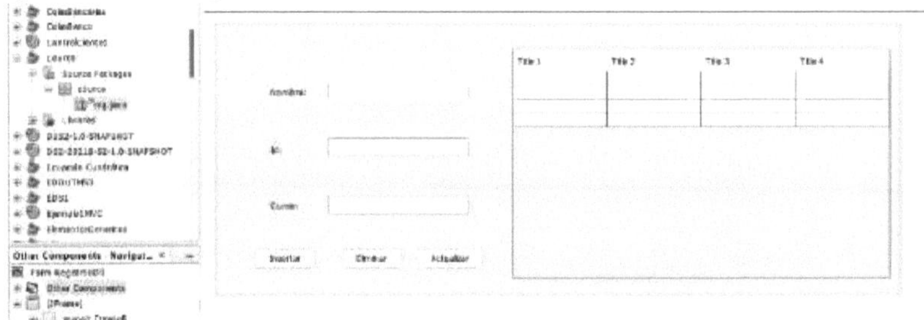

From the following links we download XAMPP and the mysql connector
XAMPP: https://mega.nz/folder/nAF3BCJA#vjGm2WjiUuX1ecgbFfLaXw
MYSQL: https://mega.nz/folder/SIVTxYxT#IkUAx3FPH82ORHMjKkqmNw
We install XAMPP
Right click on libraries

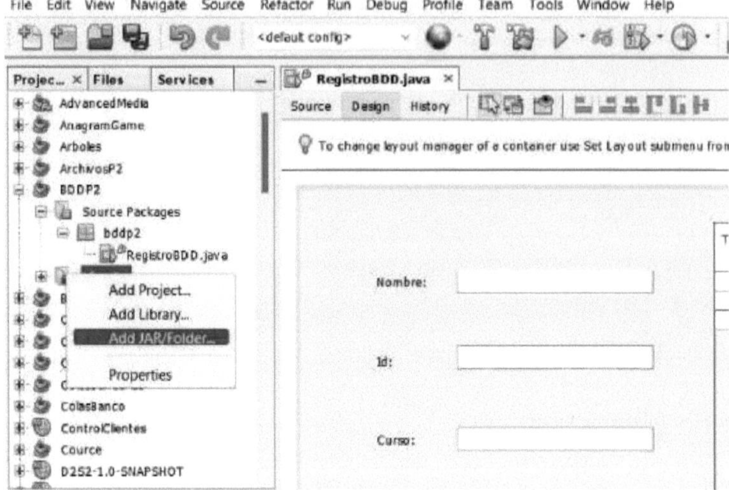

Click on Add Jar/Folder and select the downloaded connector.

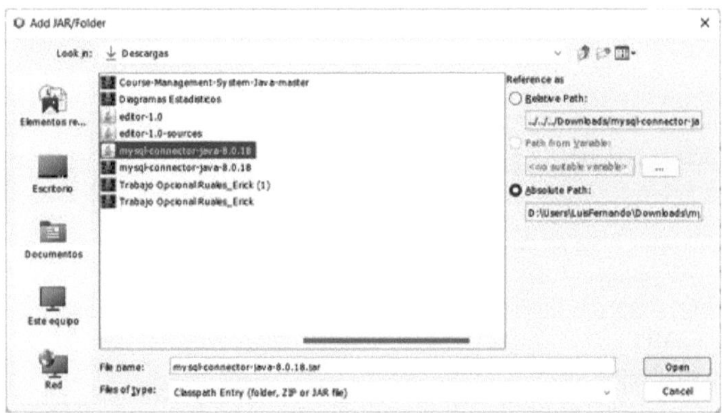

Having

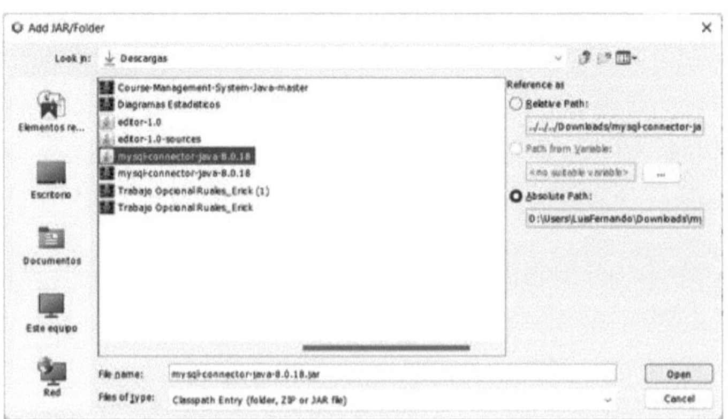

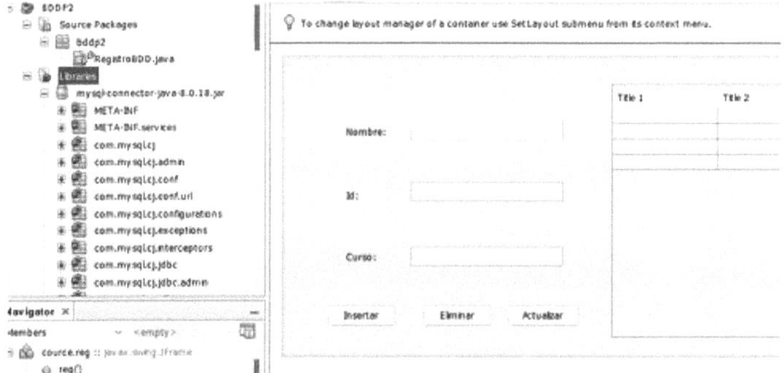

Initialise XAMPP by clicking Start in Apache and MySql.

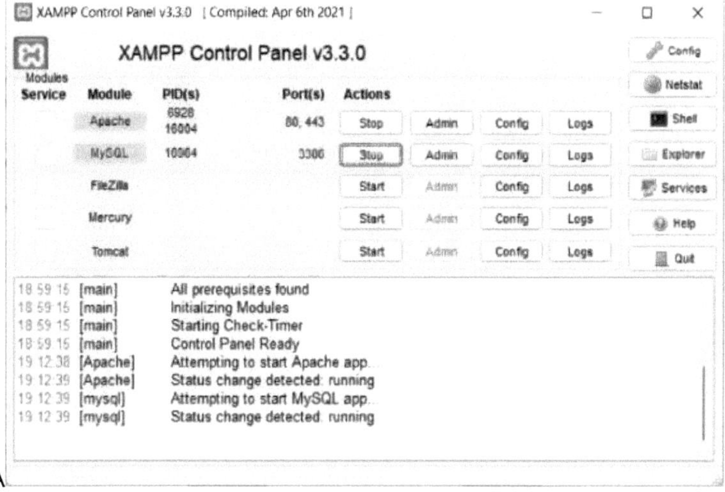

A

In the browser we place:

Click on phpMyAdmin

Click on New and enter the following name:

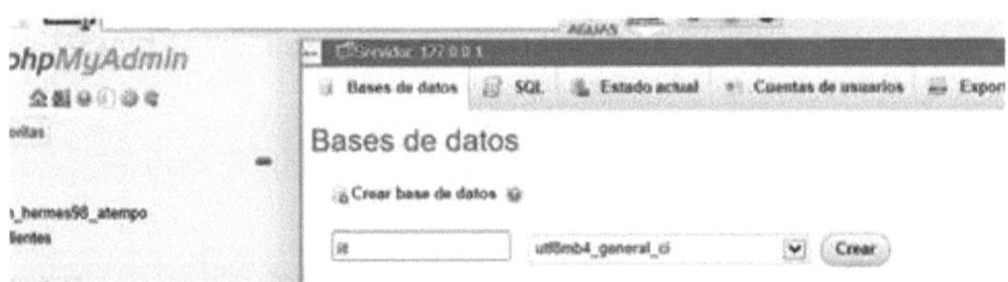

We create a table with 4 fields

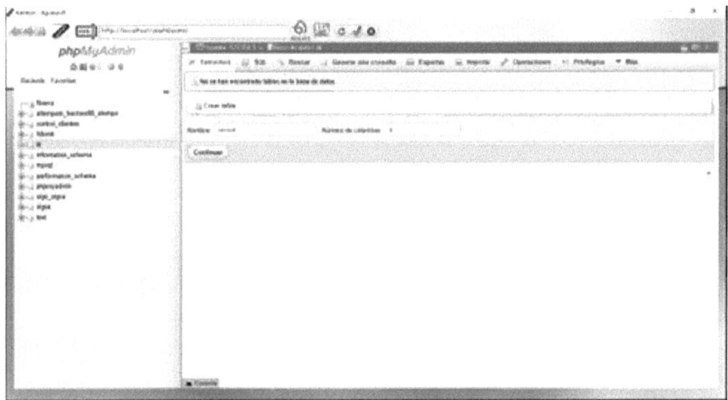

We name the fields

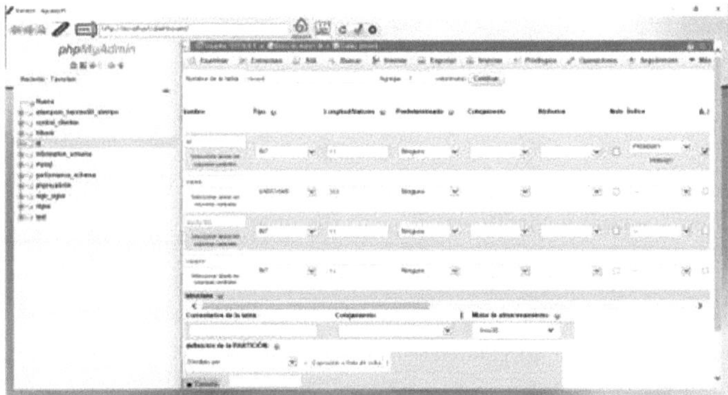

Click on save:

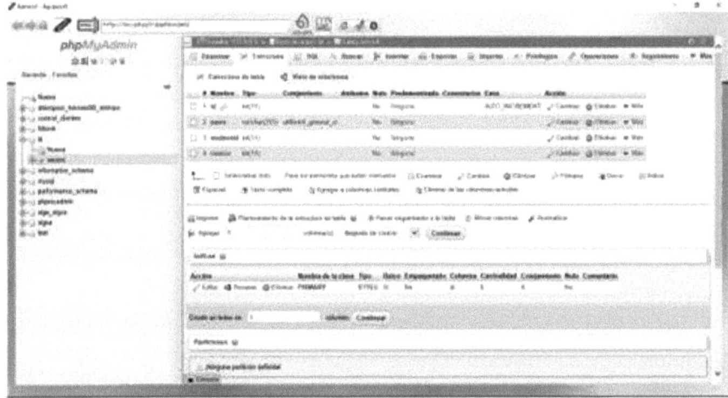

We call the library: import java.sql.*;

We create the following variables:

Connection con1;

PreparedStatement insert;

Having:

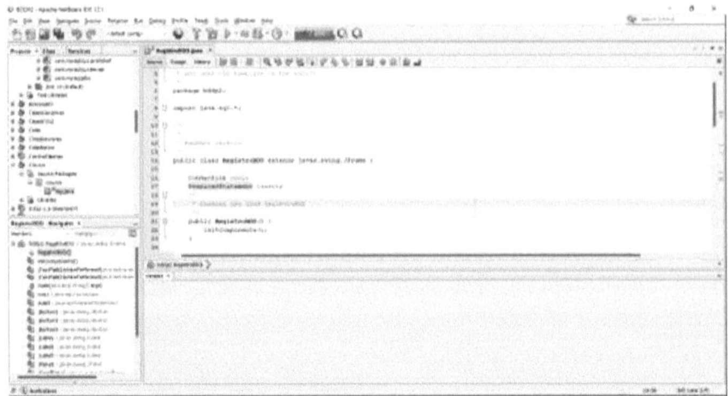

We include the following imports

```
import java.util.*;
import javax.swing.table.DefaultTableModel;
```

We create the following function:

```
private void table_update() {
int CC;
try {
Class.forName("com.mysql.jdbc.Driver");
con1 = DriverManager.getConnection("jdbc:mysql://localhost/iit", "root","");
insert = con1.prepareStatement("SELECT * FROM record");
ResultSet Rs = insert.executeQuery();
ResultSetMetaData RSMD = Rs.getMetaData();
CC = RSMD.getColumnCount();
DefaultTableModel DFT = (DefaultTableModel) jTable1.getModel();
DFT.setRowCount(0);
while (Rs.next()) {
Vector v2 = new Vector();
for (int ii = 1; ii <= CC; ii++) {
v2.add(Rs.getString("id"));
v2.add(Rs.getString("name"));
v2.add(Rs.getString("studentid"));
v2.add(Rs.getString("cource"));
}
DFT.addRow(v2);
}
} catch (Exception e) {
}
```

Having:

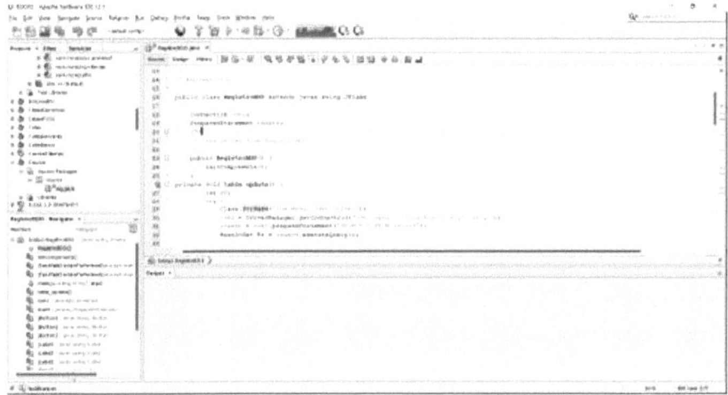

In the constructor, we place:

public RegistroBDD() { initComponents(); table_update();
}

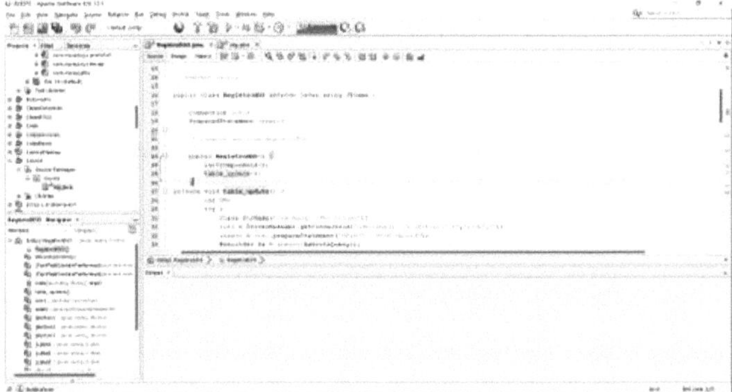

Double click on the insert button:

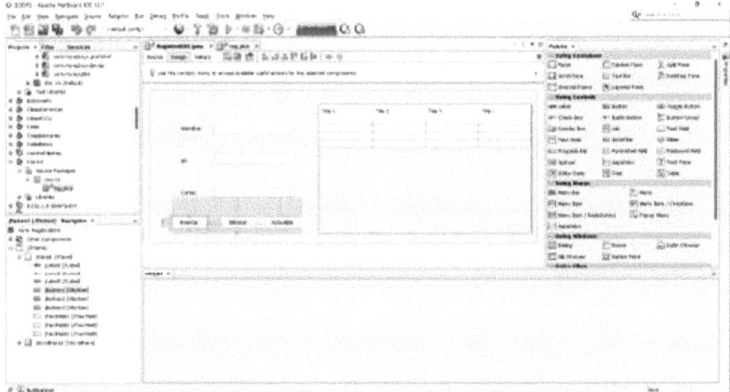

And we place the following code:

String name =jTextField1.getText();
String studentId =jTextField2.getText();

```
String cource =jTextField3.getText();
try {
Class.forName("com.mysql.jdbc.Driver");
con1 = DriverManager.getConnection("jdbc:mysql://localhost/iit", "root","");
insert = con1.prepareStatement("insert into record(name,studentid,cource)values(?,??,?)");
insert.setString(1, name);
insert.setString(2, studentId);
insert.setString(3, cource);
insert.executeUpdate();
JOptionPane.showMessageDialog(this, "Record Saved");
jTextField1.setText("");
jTextField2.setText("");
jTextField3.setText("");
jTextField1.requestFocus();
table_update();
} catch (ClassNotFoundException ex) {
Logger.getLogger(LogBDD.class.getName()).log(Level.SEVERE, null, ex);
} catch (SQLException ex) {
Logger.getLogger(LogBDD.class.getName()).log(Level.SEVERE, null, ex); }
```

Having:

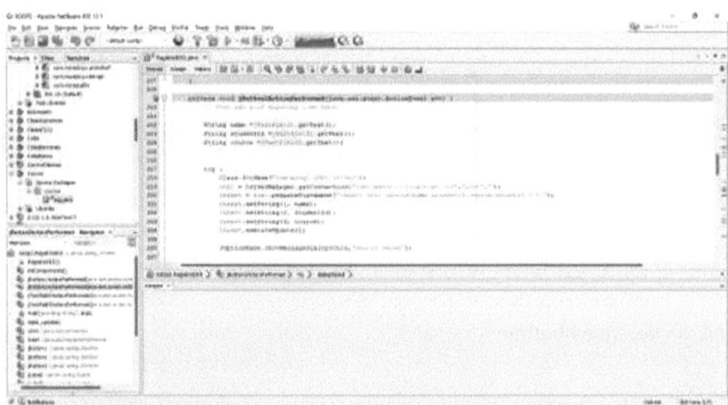

Double click on the delete button

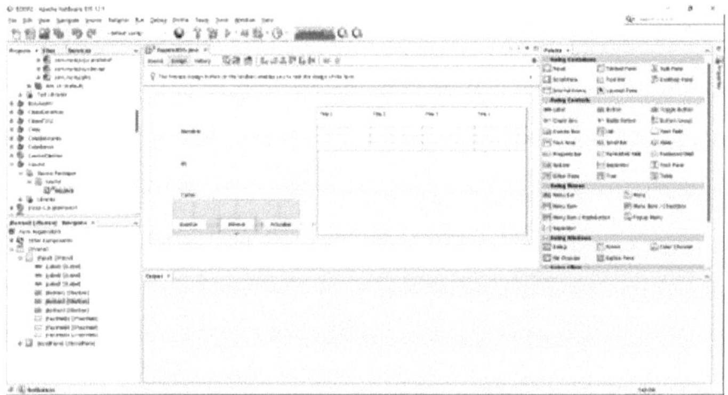

We place the following code:

```
DefaultTableModel model = (DefaultTableModel) jTable1.getModel();
int selectedIndex = jTable1.getSelectedRow();
try {
int id = Integer.parseInt(model.getValueAt(selectedIndex, 0).toString());
int dialogResult = JOptionPane.showConfirmDialog (null, "Do you want to delete the record??", "Warning",JOptionPane.YES_NO_OPTION);
if(dialogResult == JOptionPane.YES_OPTION){
Class.forName("com.mysql.jdbc.Driver");
con1 = DriverManager.getConnection("jdbc:mysql://localhost/iit", "root","");
insert = con1.prepareStatement("delete from record where id = ?");
insert.setInt(1,id);
insert.executeUpdate();
JOptionPane.showMessageDialog(this, "Record Delete");
jTextField1.setText("");
jTextField2.setText("");
jTextField3.setText("");
table_update();
}
} catch (ClassNotFoundException ex) {
} catch (SQLException ex) {
}
```

Having:

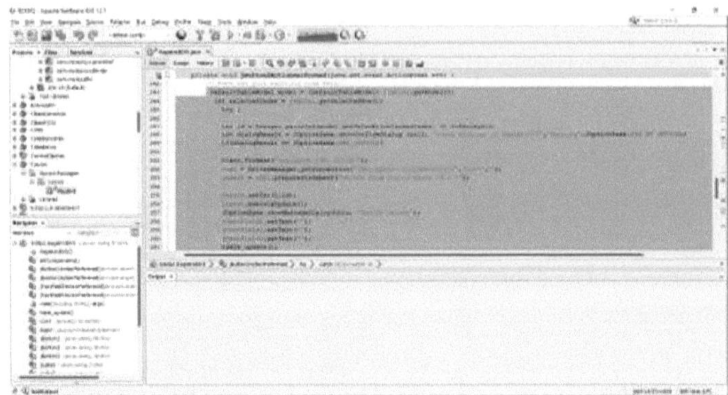

Double-click on the update button

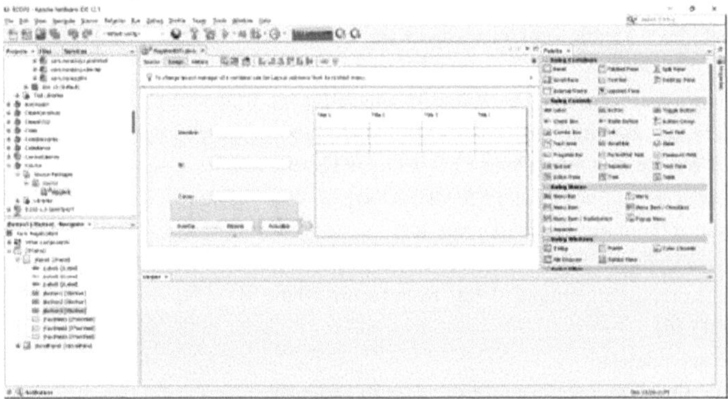

```
DefaultTableModel model = (DefaultTableModel) jTable1.getModel();
int selectedIndex = jTable1.getSelectedRow();
try {
int id = Integer.parseInt(model.getValueAt(selectedIndex, 0).toString());
String name =jTextField1.getText();
String studentId =jTextField2.getText();
String cource =jTextField3.getText();
Class.forName("com.mysql.jdbc.Driver");
con1 = DriverManager.getConnection("jdbc:mysql://localhost/iit", "root","");
insert = con1.prepareStatement("update record set name= ?,studentid= ?,cource= where id= ?");
insert.setString(1,name);
insert.setString(2,studentId);
insert.setString(3,cource);
insert.setInt(4,id);
insert.executeUpdate();
JOptionPane.showMessageDialog(this, "Record Updated");
jTextField1.setText("");
jTextField2.setText("");
```

```
jTextField3.setText("");
table_update();
} catch (ClassNotFoundException ex) {
} catch (SQLException ex) {
}
```

Having:

We activate the event

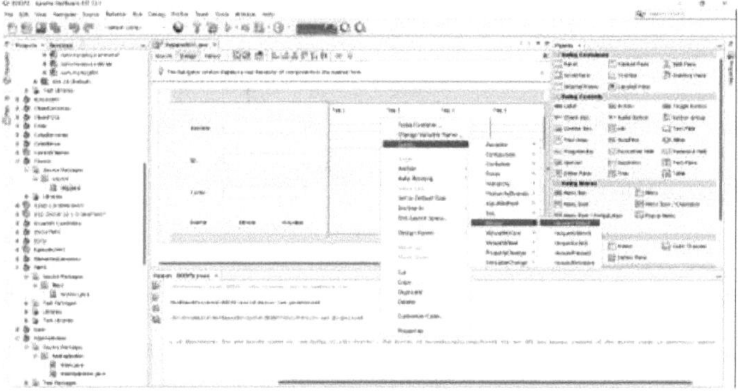

We place the following code:

```
DefaultTableModel DFT = (DefaultTableModel) jTable1.getModel();
int selectedRow = jTable1.getSelectedRow();
jTextField1.setText(DFT.getValueAt(selectedRow, 1).toString());
jTextField2.setText(DFT.getValueAt(selectedRow, 2).toString());
jTextField3.setText(DFT.getValueAt(selectedRow, 3).toString());
```

Having:

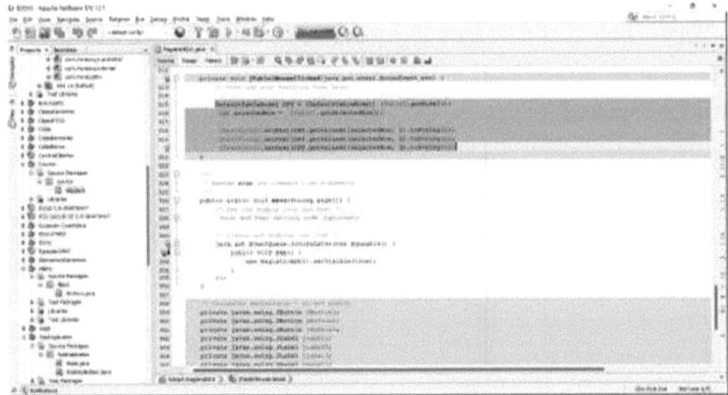

Compile and Execute:

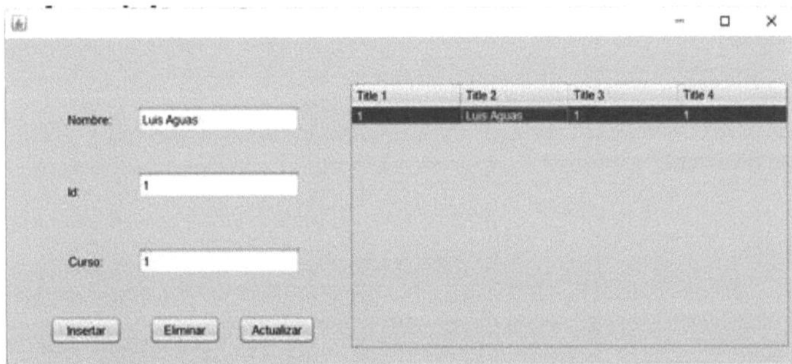

6. BIBLIOGRAPHY:

- Deitel, P., & Deitel, H. (2017). Java: How to Program (10th ed.). Pearson.
- Eckel, B. (2017). Thinking in Java (4th ed.). Prentice Hall.
- Flanagan, D. (2018). Java in a Nutshell: A Desktop Quick Reference (7th ed.). O'Reilly Media.
- Friesen, J. (2019). Java Programming for Beginners. Independently published.
- Gaddis, T. (2018). Starting Out with Java: Early Objects (6th ed.). Pearson.
- Horstmann, C. S. (2019). Core Java, Volume I: Fundamentals (12th ed.). Pearson.
- Liang, Y. D. (2019). Introduction to Java Programming and Data Structures (12th ed.). Pearson.
- Schilde, M. (2016). Java 8 in Action: Lambdas, Streams, and Functional-Style Programming. Manning Publications.
- Sharan, M. (2017). NetBeans: The Definitive Guide (2nd ed.). O'Reilly Media.
- Sierra, K., & Bates, B. (2020). Head First Java (3rd ed.). O'Reilly Media.

PRACTICE 7

1. **TOPIC:** Java Applications (Graphics)
2. **OBJECTIVES:**
- Acquire the basic concepts related to OOP.
- Recognise the characteristics of the OOP
3. **SUSTAINABLE DEVELOPMENT GOALS:**

4. **INTRODUCTION:**

Almost all Swing components and containers have an associated paint(g) method for drawing them on the screen. Java invokes this mëtodo automatically when it has to display, in a standard way, the component or container in question (i.e. its borders, its title, if it has one, etc.).

The paint(g) method is redefined when you want these elements to have a particular appearance, e.g. when you want to draw something specific on them.

The mëtodo paint(g) is of the form

```
public void paint(Graphics g) {
...
}
```

Where g is an object of the abstract class Graphics. Any container or component that can be drawn on the screen has an associated g object of this class, with the information about the area of the screen that the container or component can draw on the screen.

container or the cover component. In addition, the g-object provides methods for graphing (drawing circles, rectangles, lines, etc.).

The Graphics class is imported from awt:

import java.awt.*;

When the mëtodo paint(g) is executed it is because it has been invoked by other mëtodos, never invoked by

us, and the parameter it uses corresponds to an object of the Graphics class associated with the container or

component we are dealing with.

When redefining the paint(g) mëtodo, always start with an invocation super.paint(g) to the mëtodo of the superclass, ensuring that the standard part of the container or component we are

handling is drawn.
For example, let's draw a face in a frame. A frame is an element of the JFrame class and to draw in ël we proceed ask

```
public void paint (Graphics g){ super.paint(g);
//Drawing the outline of the face
g.setColor(Color.BLACK);
g.fillOval(105, 70, 100, 100);
//Drawing of the eyes
g.setColor(Color.GREEN);
g.fillOval(125, 100, 10, 10);
g.fillOval(175, 100, 10, 10);
//Drawing of the nose
g.drawLine(150, 100, 150, 130);
//Drawing of the mouth
g.drawArc(118, 120, 75, 30, 180, 180);
}
```

To understand what the above mëtodo it is necessary to know that:
The coordinate system of a container has its origin in its upper left corner.
The abscissae are increased to the right and the ordinates are increased downwards.
Each point is a p^xel.
In general, the drawing of a figure (rectangle, ellipse, round rectangle, etc.) is done by giving the coordinates of the upper left corner of an imaginary rectangle that contains it.
Some mëtodos of the Graphics class for drawing figures are:
drawLine(x1,y1,x2,y2): draws a straight line from point (x1,y1) to point (x2,y2)
fillRect(x,y,width,height): fills the rectangle having its top left corner at (x,y) and the given width and length
drawOval(x,y,width,height): draws an ellipse contained in an imaginary rectangle whose top left corner is at (x,y) and has the given width and length fillOval(x,y,width,height): fills the ellipse specified bydrawOval(x,y,width,length) drawArc(x,y,width,height, startAngle,sweepAngle): draws part of an ellipse inside an imaginary rectangle whose top left corner is at (x,y), has the given length and width, starts drawing at the startAngle angle and does a sweep sweepAngle setColor(Color.red): changes the "ink" of object g to red. The Color class is imported from awt:
import java.awt.*;
Drawing on panels
When a component is updated, its current appearance is erased and paint(g) is invoked. Pre-erase can cause flickering, so sometimes the paint(g) method avoids doing this.
However, the actualization may need to pre-sweep (to update the background of the component, for example). In these cases, the mëtodo paintComponent(g) of the JComponent class is invoked, which allows to pre-sweep, but using the double buffer technique to remove the flicker.
In cases like the above what is done is to redefine the mëtodo paintComponent(g) instead of the mëtodo paint(g).
For example, to draw the face we painted before, but on a (j)panel instead of a frame, we do the following:
The class PanelFace, which extends the class JPanel, is declared as a (private) class of the

class MarcoCara that we created before.

We redefine the mëtodo paintComponent(g) using the same instructions as before, but initially calling super.paintComponent(g)

public void paintComponent(Graphics g) { super.paintComponent(g);...}

When the content of a frame or panel changes, the repaint() mëtodo is responsible for updating the container and displaying it on the screen, by invoking impHcitly the paint(g) or paintComponent(g) mëtodo.

For example, to add a button to the frame showing a smiley face so that, when pressed, the face changes to a smiley face, simply do the following:

Add to contentPane the button whose effect will change the smile of the face Add a boolean attribute to the frame that indicates whether the face is smiling or not private boolean smile=true;

Inside the actionPerformed of the button we code the following: smile=!smile;

repaint();

The mëtodo paintComponent(g) for painting the panel is redefined as follows: public void paintComponent(Graphics g) {

super.paintComponent(g);

//Drawing of the face as before, except for the mouth

//Drawing of the mouth

if (smile) g.drawArc(118, 125, 75, 75, 30, 180, 180);

else g.drawArc(118, 125, 75, 30, 180, -180);

}

Draw text

The Graphics class allows to "draw" text, as an alternative to the text displayed in the JLabel, JTextField and JTextArea components. The mëtodo that allows to draw text on the JFrame is:

drawString(String str, int x, int y);

Class Colour

The java.awt.Color class encapsulates colours using the RGB (Red, Green, Blue) format. The components of each primary colour in the resulting colour are expressed as integers between 0 and 255, with 0 being the minimum intensity of that colour and 255 being the maximum. In the Color class there are constants for frequently used default colours: black, white, green, blue, red, yellow, magenta, cyan, orange, pink, gray, darkGray, lightGray.

Presentation of images

Java allows you to incorporate GIF and JPEG images defined in files. The java.awt.Image class is available for this purpose. To load an image you have to indicate the location of the file and load it using the mëtodo getImage(). This mëtodo exists in the classes java.awt.Toolkit.

So, to load an image you have to start by creating an Image object (or a reference) and call the mëtodo getImage() (from Toolkit); Once the image is loaded, you have to render it, for which the mëtodo paint() is redefined to call the mëtodo drawImage() of the Graphics class. Graphics objects can display images through the mëtodo: drawImage(). This mëtodo supports several forms, although it is almost always necessary to include the name of the created image object.

Image Class

An image is a rectangular graphic object composed of coloured pixels. Each pixel in an image describes a colour of a particular location in the image.

Here are some mëtodos of the Image class:

The Graphics class provides the mëtodo drawImage() for drawing images; this mëtodo supports several forms:

- drawImage (Image i, int x, int y, ImageObserver o)
- drawImage (Image i,int x,int y,int width,int height,ImageObserver o)

An example of the paint(Graphics G) method for fetching an image from the root folder is as follows:

```
public void paint (Graphics g) {
super.paint(g);
Toolkit t = Toolkit.getDefaultToolkit ();
Image image = t.getImage ("image1.jpg"); g.drawImage (image, 0, 0, this);
}
```

5. DEVELOPMENT:

<u>HIERARCHICAL RELATIONSHIP</u>

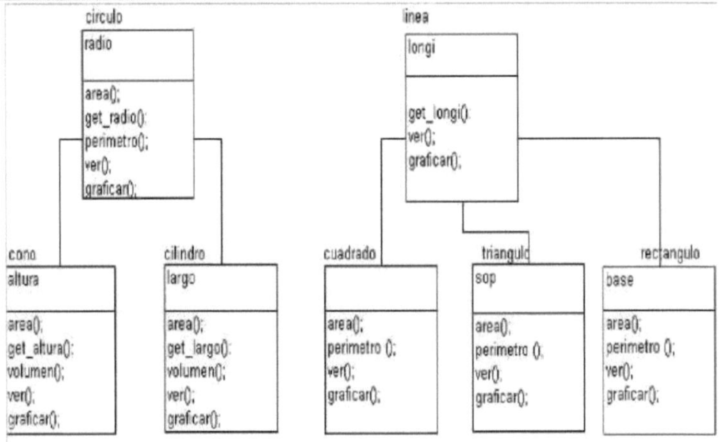

- Log in to Netbeans

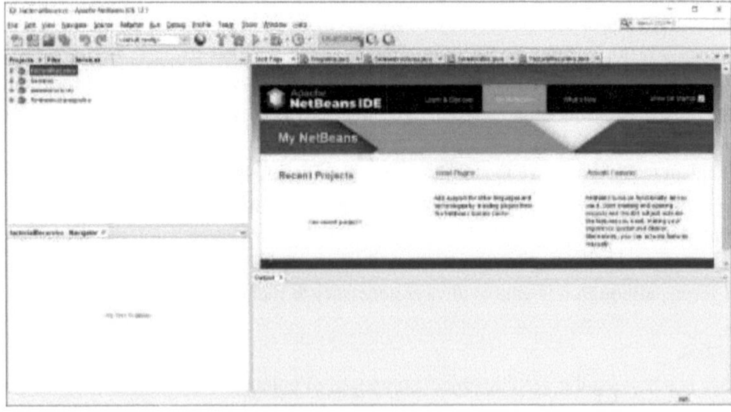

- We create a new project:

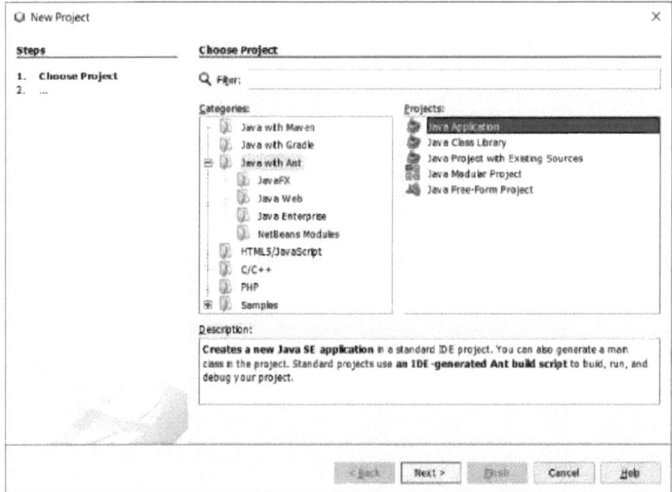

- We place as name

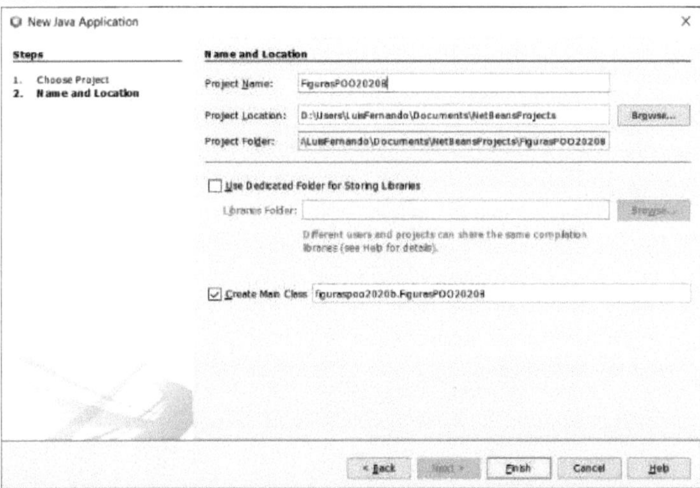

Click Finish

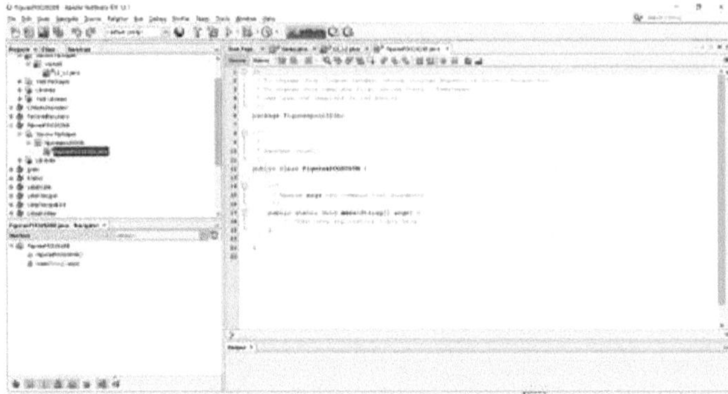

Click on delete

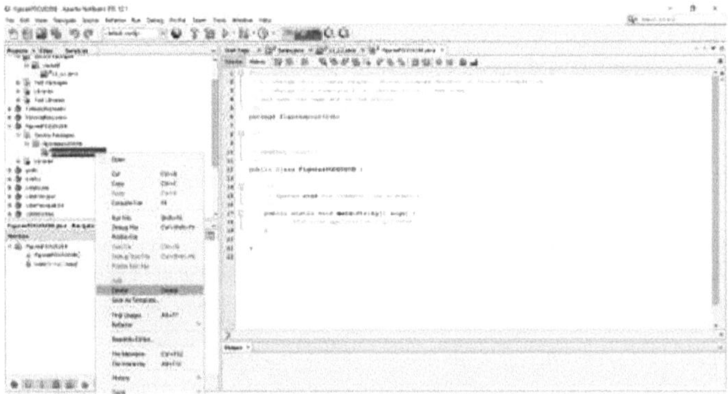

Then Click on Refactor

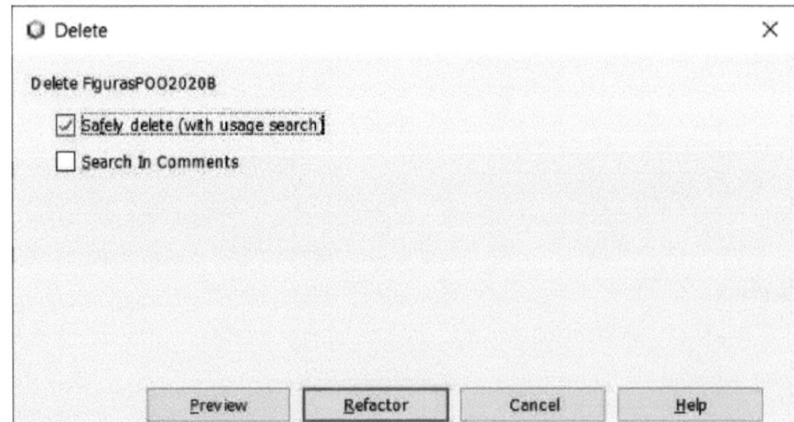

For the Lmea:

We create the class Line

```
import java.awt.*;
public class Line{
protected int longi;
public Linea(int longi){ this.longi=longi;
}
public int get_longi(){ return longi;
}
public void set_longi(int longi){ this.longi=longi;
}
public void graph(Graphics Cl, Line cl, int x, int y){
Cl.setColor(Color.green);
Cl.drawLine(x,y+cl.get_longi()/2,x,y+cl.get_longi()+cl.get_longi()/2);
}
public void ver(Graphics Cl, Line cl, int x, int y){
Font type1=new Font("Arial", Font.BOLD+Font.ITALIC,14);
Font type2=new Font("Comic Sans MS", Font.ITALIC,13);
Cl.setFont(type1);
Cl.setColor(Color.black);
Cl.drawString("Lmea",x+255,y+180);
Cl.setColor(Color.blue);
Cl.setFont(type2);
Cl.drawString("Length: "+cl.get_longi()+" cm",x+255,y+305);
}
}///end of class line
```

Having:

For Cuadrado:

Then we create the class Square based on the previous process, with the following code:

```
import java.awt.*;
/**
*
* @author LuisFernando
*/
public class Square extends Line{
public Square (int longi){
super(longi);
}
public void graph(Graphics Cl,int x, int y){
Cl.setColor(Color.blue);
Cl.fillRect(x,y,super.get_longi(),super.get_longi()-1);
}
public double perimeter(){
return 4*(super.get_longi());
}
public double area(){
return java.lang.Math.pow(super.get_longi(),2);
}
public void ver(Graphics Cl,Square cu,int x, int y){
Font type1=new Font("Arial", Font.BOLD+Font.ITALIC,14);
Font type2=new Font("Comic Sans MS", Font.ITALIC,13);
Cl.setFont(type1);
Cl.setColor(Color.black);
Cl.drawString("Square",x+480,y);
Cl.setColor(Color.blue);
Cl.setFont(type2);
Cl.drawString("Side: "+super.get_longi()+" cm",x+480,y+110);
```

```
Cl.drawString("Perimeter: "+cu.perimeter()+" cm",x+480,y+125);
Cl.drawString("Area: "+cu.area()+" cm2 ",x+480,y+140);
}
}///end square class
```
Having:

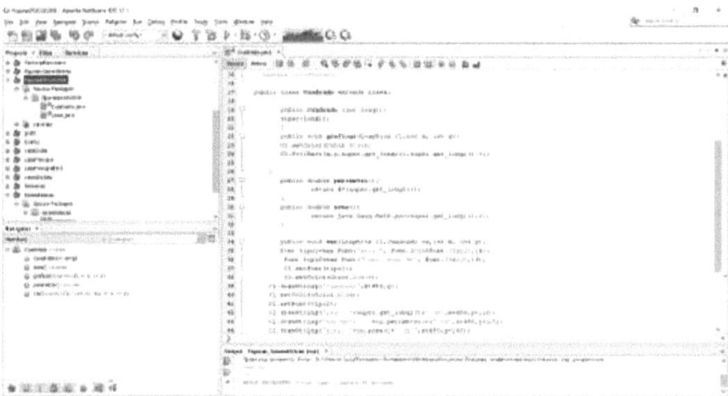

For the Circle:

We create the class Circle

```
import java.awt.*;
/**
*
* @author LuisFernando
*/
public class Circle {
protected int radio;
public Circle(int radius)
{
this.radio=radio;
}///end circle
public int get_radius(){
return radio;
}///end get_radio
public void set_radio(int radius)
{
this.radio=radio;
}///end set
public void graph(Graphics Cl,Circle cl,int x, int y)
{
Cl.setColor(Color.red);
Cl.fillOval(x,y+15,cl.get_radius()*4,cl.get_radius()*4);
}///end plot
public double area(){
```

```
return java.lang.Math.PI*java.lang.Math.pow(this.radius,2);
}///end area
public double perimeter(){
return 2*java.lang.Math.PI*this.radius;
}
public void ver(Graphics Cl, Circle cl, int x, int y){
Font type1=new Font("Arial", Font.BOLD+Font.ITALIC,14);
Font type2=new Font("Comic Sans MS", Font.ITALIC,13);
Cl.setFont(type1);
Cl.setColor(Color.black);
Cl.drawString("Circle",x,y);
Cl.setColor(Color.blue);
Cl.setFont(type2);
Cl.drawString("Radius: "+cl.get_radius()+" cm",x,y+110);
Cl.drawString("Perimeter: "+cl.perimeter()+" cm",x,y+125);
Cl.drawString("Area: "+cl.area()+" cm2 ",x,y+140);
}
}///end class circle
```

Having:

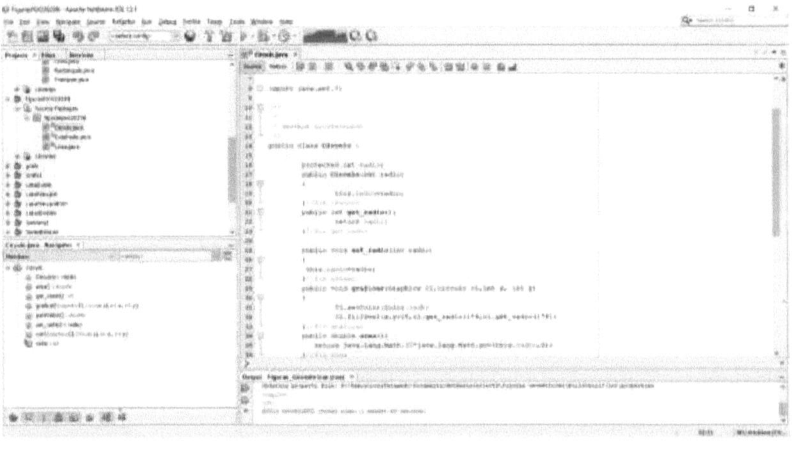

For the Rectangle:

We create the class Rectangle

```
import java.awt.*;
public class Rectangle extends Linea{ int base;
public Rectangle(int base, int longi){ super(longi);
this.base=base;
}
public int get_base(){
return base;
}
public void ver(Graphics Cl,Rectangle rec,int x, int y){
```

```
Font type1=new Font("Arial", Font.BOLD+Font.ITALIC,14);
Font type2=new Font("Comic Sans MS", Font.ITALIC,13);
Cl.setFont(type1);
Cl.setColor(Color.black);
Cl.drawString("Rectangle",x+480,y+180);
Cl.setColor(Color.blue);
Cl.setFont(type2);
Cl.drawString("Height: "+super.get_longi()+" cm",x+480,y+305);
Cl.drawString("Base: "+rec.get_base()+" cm",x+480,y+320);
Cl.drawString("Perimeter: "+rec.perimeter()+" cm",x+480,y+335);
Cl.drawString("Area: "+rec.area()+" cm^2 ",x+480,y+350);
}
public double perimeter(){
return (2*(super.get_longi())+2*this.base);
}
public double area(){
return (this.base*super.get_longi())/2;
}
public void graph(Graphics Cl,int x, int y){
Cl.setColor(Color.orange);
Cl.fillRect(x,y,super.get_longi()*2,this.base*4);
} //end rectangle class
```

Having:

For the Triangle:

We create the Triangle class

```
import java.awt.*;
/**
*
* @author LuisFernando
*/
public class Triangle extends Line{
private int sop;
public Triangulo(int sop, int longi){
```

```
super(longi);
this.sop=sop;
}
public void graph(Graphics Cl, Triangle cl,int x, int y)
{
int x1 []={x,x-(cl.get_sop()/2)*3,x+(cl.get_sop()/2)*3};
int y1 []={y,y+super.get_longi()*3,y+cl.get_longi()*3};
Cl.setColor(Color.pink);
Cl.fillPolygon(x1,y1,3);
}///end plot
public int get_sop(){
return sop;
}
public void ver(Graphics Cl,Triangle tri,int x, int y){
Font type1=new Font("Arial", Font.BOLD+Font.ITALIC,14);
Font type2=new Font("Comic Sans MS", Font.ITALIC,13);
Cl.setFont(type1);
Cl.setColor(Color.black);
Cl.drawString("Triangle",x+625,y);
Cl.setColor(Color.blue);
Cl.setFont(type2);
Cl.drawString("Height: "+super.get_longi()+" cm",x+625,y+180);
Cl.drawString("Base: "+tri.get_sop()+ " cm",x+625,y+195);
Cl.drawString("Area: "+tri.area()+" cm² ",x+625,y+210);
}
public double area(){
return (super.get_longi()*this.sop)/2;
}
}///end triangle class
```

Having

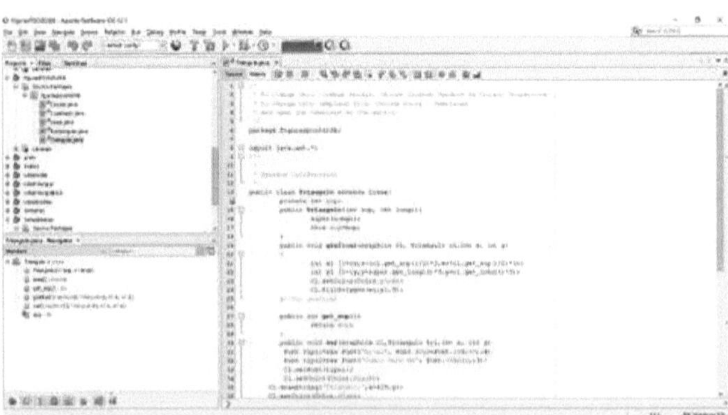

For the Cylinder:

We create the class Cylinder import java.awt.*;

```
/**
*
* @author LuisFernando
*/
public class Cylinder extends Circle{
private int long;
public Cylinder(int radius,int length){
super(radio);
this.length=length;
}
public int get_length(){ return length;
}
public void ver(Graphics Cl, Cylinder cl, int x, int y){
Font type1=new Font("Arial", Font.BOLD+Font.ITALIC,14);
Font type2=new Font("Comic Sans MS", Font.ITALIC,13);
Cl.setFont(type1);
Cl.setColor(Color.black);
Cl.drawString("Cylinder",x+255,y);
Cl.setColor(Color.blue);
Cl.setFont(type2);
Cl.drawString("Radius: "+super.get_radius()+" cm",x+255,y+110);
Cl.drawString("Height: "+cl.get_length()+" cm",x+255,y+125);
Cl.drawString("Area: "+cl.area()+" cm2 ",x+255,y+140);
Cl.drawString("Volume: "+cl.volume()+" cm3 ",x+255,y+155);
}
public double volume(){
return super.area()*this.length;
}
public double area(){
return (super.area()+super.perimeter()*this.length);
}
public void graph(Graphics Cl,Cylinder cl,int x, int y){
Cl.setColor(Color.cyan);
Cl.fillOval(x,y,super.get_radius()*2,super.get_radius());
Cl.fillOval(x,y+cl.get_length(),super.get_radius()*2,super.get_radius());
Cl.drawLine(x,y+super.get_radius()/2,x,y+cl.get_length()+super.get_radius()/2);
Cl.drawLine(x+super.get_radius()*2,y+super.get_radius()/2,x+super.get_radius()*2,y+cl.get_
lar go()+super.get_radius()/2);
}
}///end cylinder class
```

Having:

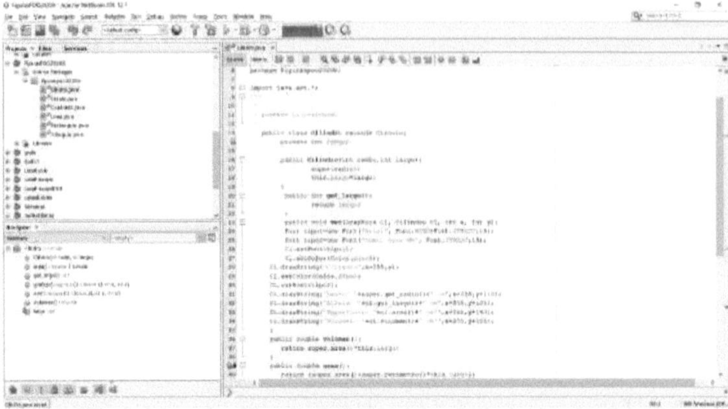

For the Cone:

We create the Cone class

```
import java.awt.*;
/**
*
* @author LuisFernando
*/
public class Cone extends Circle{ private int height;
public Cone(int radius, int height){
super(radio);
this.height=height;
}
public int get_height(){
return height;
}
public void set_height(){
this.height=height;
}
public void graph(Graphics Cl,Cone cl,int x, int y){
Cl.setColor(Color.yellow);
Cl.fillOval(x,y,super.get_radius()*4,super.get_radius()*2);
Cl.drawLine(x,y+super.get_radius(),x+super.get_radius()*2,y+cl.get_height()+super.get_radi
us() );
Cl.drawLine(x+super.get_radius()*4,y+super.get_radius(),x+super.get_radius()*2,y+cl.get_al
tur a()+super.get_radius());
}
public void ver(Graphics Cl, Cone cl, int x, int y){
Font type1=new Font("Arial", Font.BOLD+Font.ITALIC,14);
Font type2=new Font("Comic Sans MS", Font.ITALIC,13);
Cl.setFont(type1);
Cl.setColor(Color.black);
```

```
Cl.drawString("Cone",x,y+180);
Cl.setColor(Color.blue);
Cl.setFont(type2);
Cl.drawString("Radius: "+super.get_radius()+" cm",x,y+305);
Cl.drawString("Height: "+cl.get_height()+" cm",x,y+320);
Cl.drawString("Surface: "+cl.surface(cl)+" cm2 ",x,y+335);
Cl.drawString("Volume: "+cl.volume(cl)+" cm3 ",x,y+350);
}
public double volume(Cone cl){
return (super.area()*cl.get_height())/3;
}
public double surface(Cone cl){
return (super.area()+2*java.lang.Math.PI*cl.get_height()+super.perimeter());
}
}///end cone
```

Having:

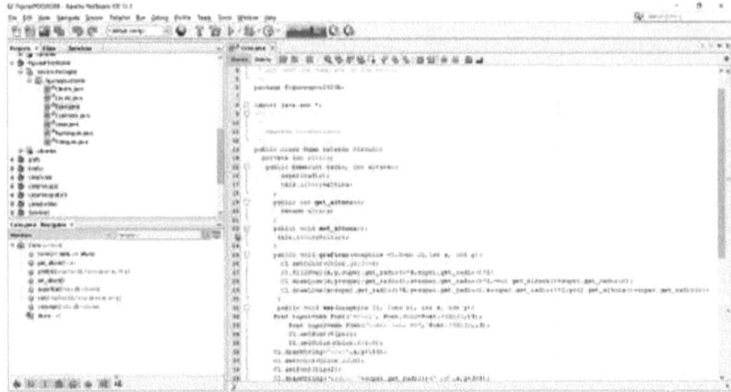

We create a jFrame

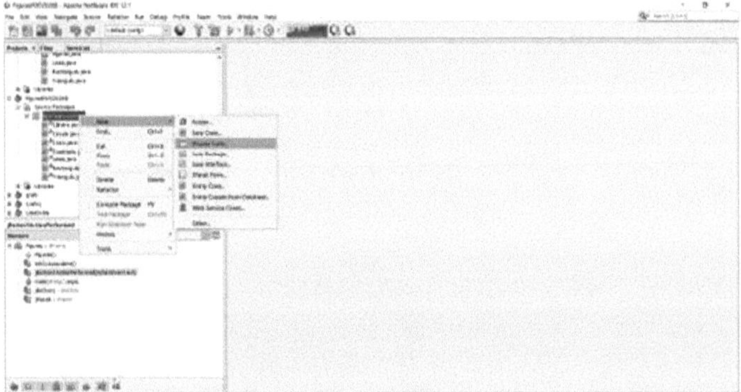

We place the following name:

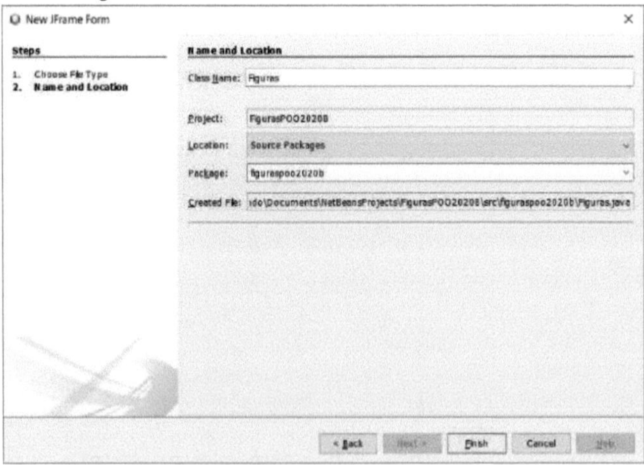

Having:

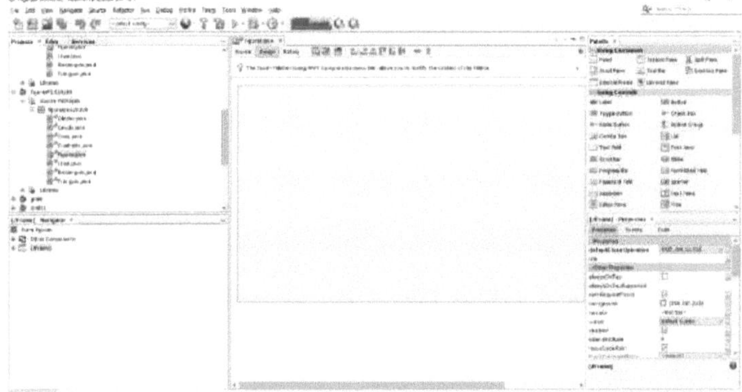

From the Pallete, we choose a jButton and a jPanel, having:

Select the jPanel and go to properties to background

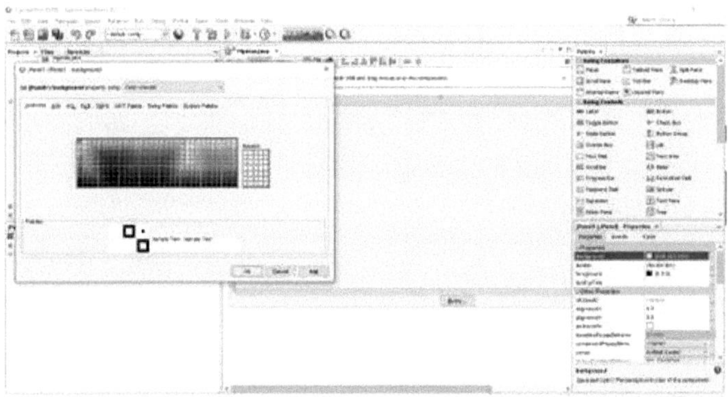

Having

Then we select the jButton and go to properties

Double click on the button

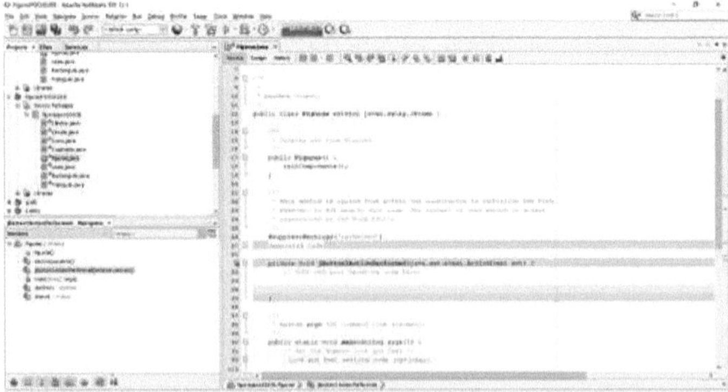

We place this code

private void jButton1ActionPerformed(java.awt.event.ActionEvent evt) { // TODO add your

```
handling code here:
int hori=20; int vert=40;
Graphics Cl=jPanel1.getGraphics();
Circle cir = new Circle(20);
Cone con= new Cone(20,70);
Cylinder cil= new Cylinder(20,60);
Line lin=new Line(60);
Square cua= new Square(80);
Rectangle rec= new Rectangle(20,60);
Triangle tri= new Triangle(30,50);
cir.view(Cl,cir,hori,vert); cir.plot(Cl,cir,hori,vert);
con.ver(Cl,con,hori,vert);
con.plot(Cl,con,hori,vert+200);
cyl.plot(Cl,cyl,hori+255,vert+15);
cil.ver(Cl,cil,hori,vert);
qua.plot(Cl,hori+480,vert+15);
cua.ver(Cl,cua,hori,vert);
rec.ver(Cl,rec,hori,vert);
rec.plot(Cl,hori+480,vert+200);
lin.plot(Cl,lin,hori+255,vert+200);
lin.ver(Cl,lin,hori,vert);
tri.ver(Cl,tri,hori,vert);
tri.plot(Cl, tri,hori+680,vert+15);
```

Having:

We compile and run:

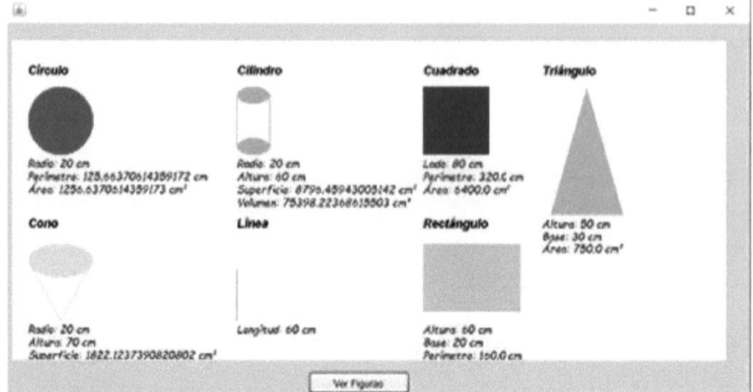

6. BIBLIOGRAPHY:

- Deitel, P., & Deitel, H. (2017). Java: How to Program (10th ed.). Pearson.
- Eckel, B. (2017). Thinking in Java (4th ed.). Prentice Hall.
- Flanagan, D. (2018). Java in a Nutshell: A Desktop Quick Reference (7th ed.). O'Reilly Media.
- Friesen, J. (2019). Java Programming for Beginners. Independently published.
- Gaddis, T. (2018). Starting Out with Java: Early Objects (6th ed.). Pearson.
- Horstmann, C. S. (2019). Core Java, Volume I: Fundamentals (12th ed.). Pearson.
- Liang, Y. D. (2019). Introduction to Java Programming and Data Structures (12th ed.). Pearson.
- Schilde, M. (2016). Java 8 in Action: Lambdas, Streams, and Functional-Style Programming. Manning Publications.
- Sharan, M. (2017). NetBeans: The Definitive Guide (2nd ed.). O'Reilly Media.
- Sierra, K., & Bates, B. (2020). Head First Java (3rd ed.). O'Reilly Media.

PRACTICE 8

1. **TOPIC:** Java Applications (Bar and Pie Diagrams)
2. **OBJECTIVES:**

- Acquire the basic concepts related to OOP.
- Recognise the characteristics of the OOP

3. **SUSTAINABLE DEVELOPMENT GOALS:**

4. **INTRODUCTION:**

Classes and objects

- Object

An object is a generic encapsulation of data and the procedures to manipulate it.

Like real-world objects, software objects have state and behaviour. The state of objects is determined by one or more *variables* and the behaviour by the implementation of *methods*.

The following figure shows the common representation of the software objects

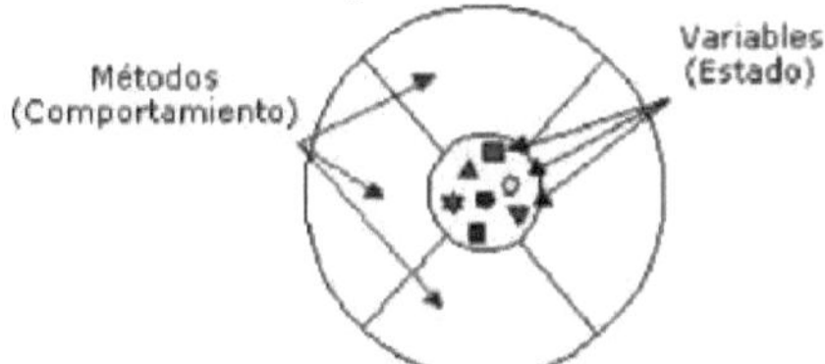

As can be seen in the figure, all objects have a public part (their behaviour) and a private part (their state). In this case, we made a cross-sectional view but from the outside world, the object will be observed as a sphere.

• Clase

A class consists of the *methods* and *variables* that define the characteristics common to all objects of that class.

The key to OOP is to abstract the methods and data common to a set of objects and store them in a class.

Class X

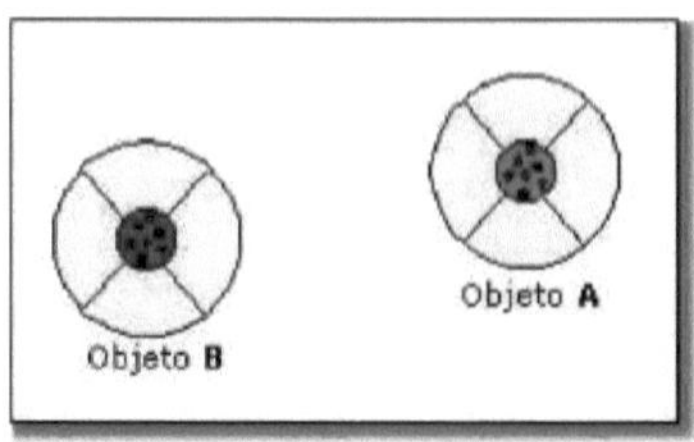

In the figure above, object A and object B are instances of class X.
Each of the objects has its own copy of the variables defined in the class from which it is instantiated and shares the same implementation of the methods.

5. DEVELOPMENT:

"Netbeans login

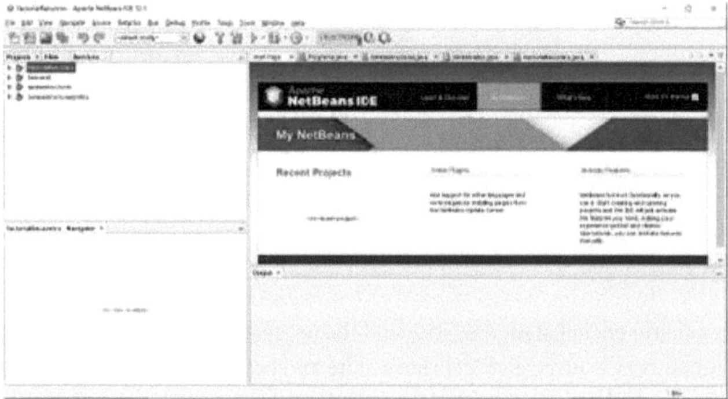

"We created a new project:

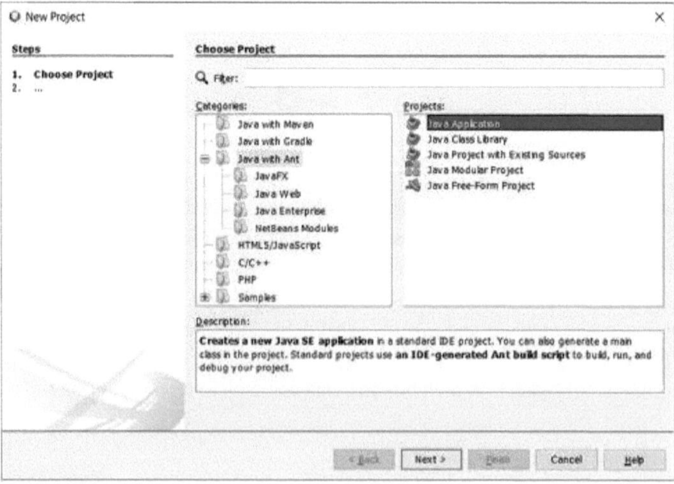

"We place as name
Engineering Science

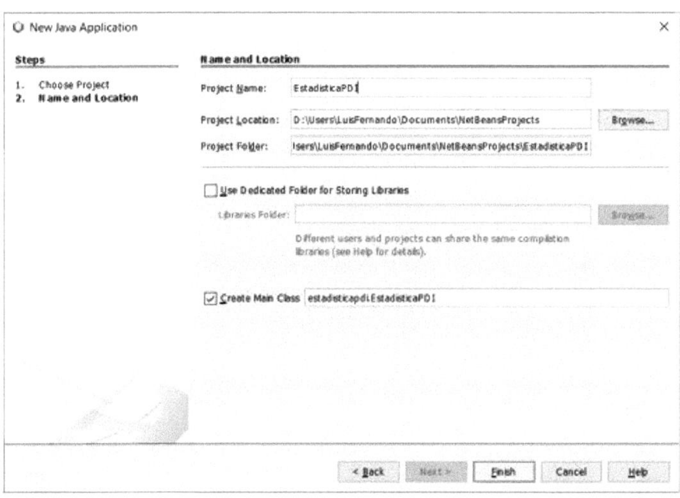

"Click on Finish

"We delete the class that was created by default.

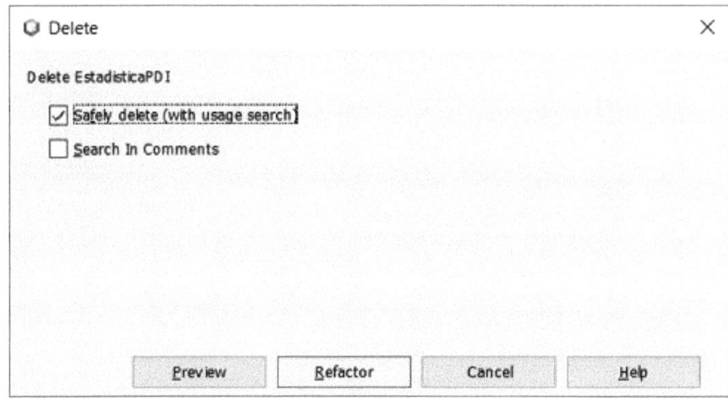

- Having

- Click on add JFrame

"We place the following name

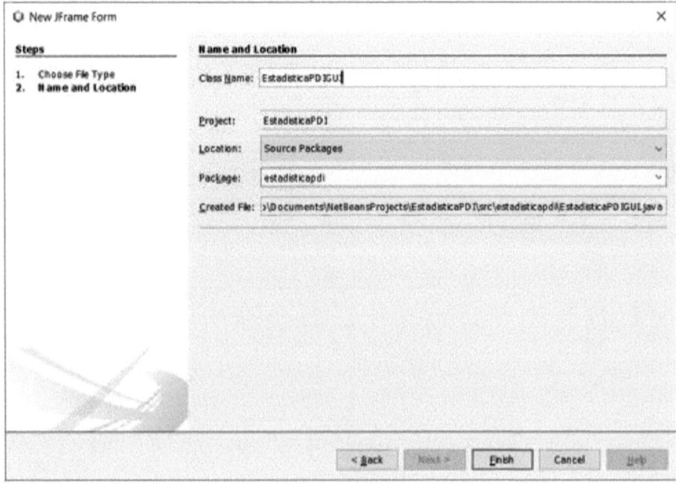

"Click on Finish

- Having

"We create the following interface

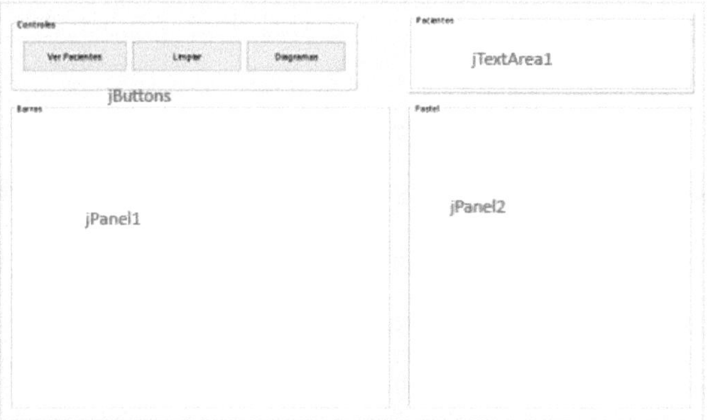

"We create the following class:

"With the following name:

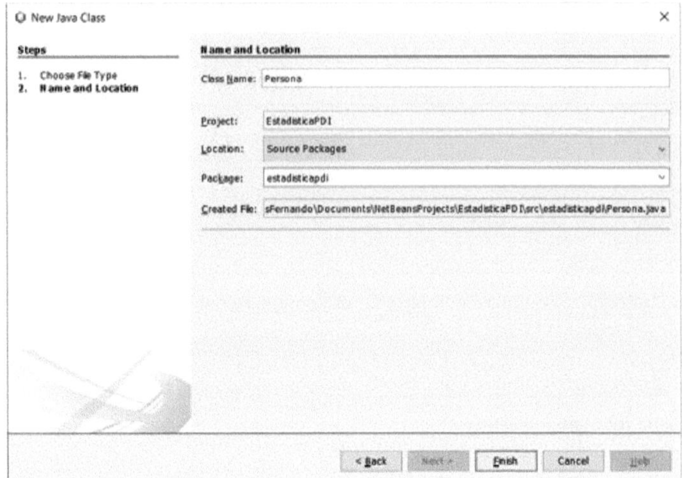

"Having:

- We place the following code:

```
public class Person {
protected String cedula; protected String nombre;
public Person(String ID,String name)
{
this.name=firstname; this.ID=cedula;
}///end person
public String get_cedula()
{
return cedula;
}// end get_cedula
public String get_name()
{
return name;
```

```
}
public void setea_datos( String cedula,String nombre) {
this.name=name; this.cedula=cedula;
}///end setea_data
}
```

- Having:

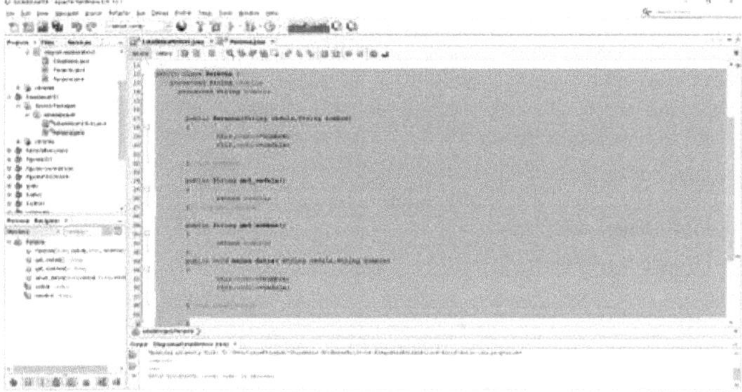

- We create another class, with the following name:

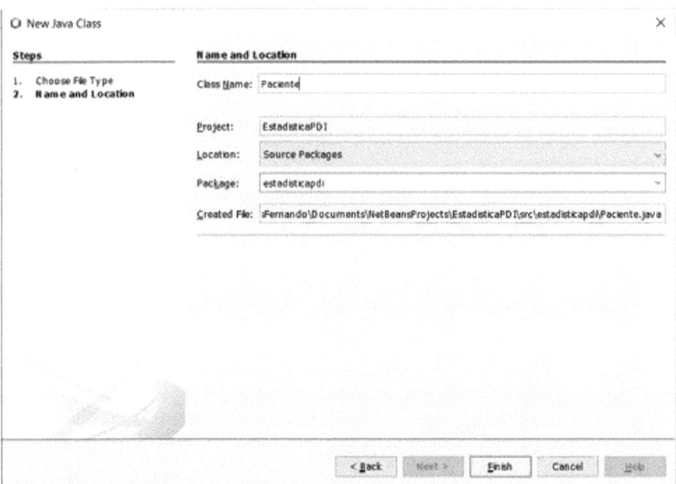

- Having:

We place the following code:

```
public class Patient extends Person{
String illness;
String safe;
public Paciente(String cedula,String nombre,String enfermedad,String seguro ) {
super(ID, name);
this.disease=disease; this.insurance=insurance;
}
public String get_disease()
{
return illness;
}// end get_cedula
public String get_insurance()
{
return safe;
}// end get_cedula
}
```

- Having:

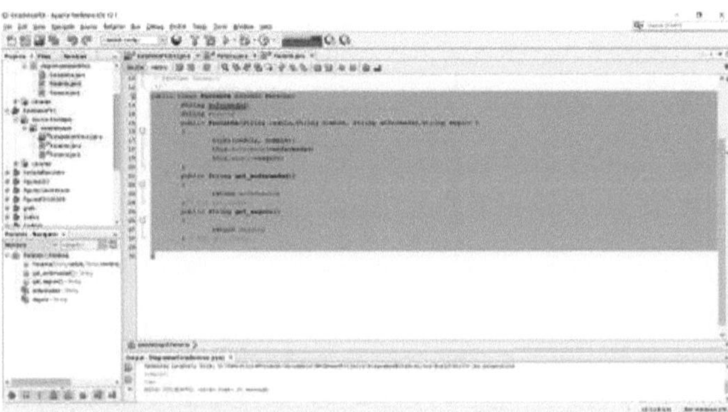

- We declare the following variables

```
Patient A[]=new Patient[3];
Font type1 =new Font("Arial",Font.BOLD+Font.ITALIC,14);
Font type2 =new Font("Comic Sans MS",Font.ITALIC,13);
```

- Having:

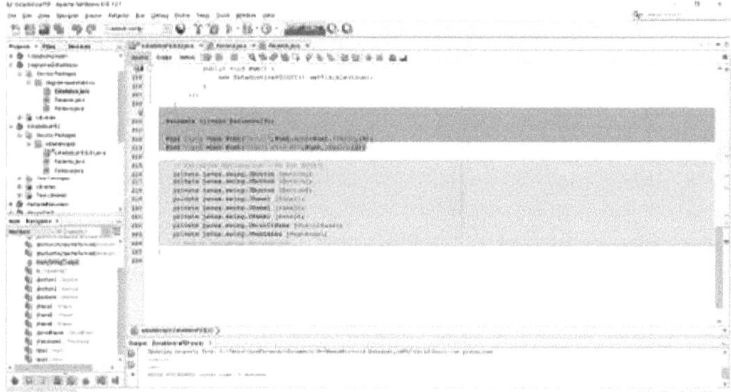

- Double click on the following button

- We place the following code:

```
A[0]=new Patient ("1716866916", "Luis Aguas", "None", "Insurance");
A[1]=new Patient ("1716866916", "Fabiola Aguas", "None", "Insurance");
A[2]=new Patient ("1716866916", "Sofia Aguas", "None", "Not sure");
jTextArea1.append("\nCëdula - Surname and First Names - Disease - Insurance");
jTextArea1.append("\n ");
for (int i=0;i<A.length;i++)
jTextArea1.append("+A[i].get_cedula()+"-"+A[i].get_name()+"-"+A[i].get_disease()+"-
"+A[i].get_insurance());
```

- Having:

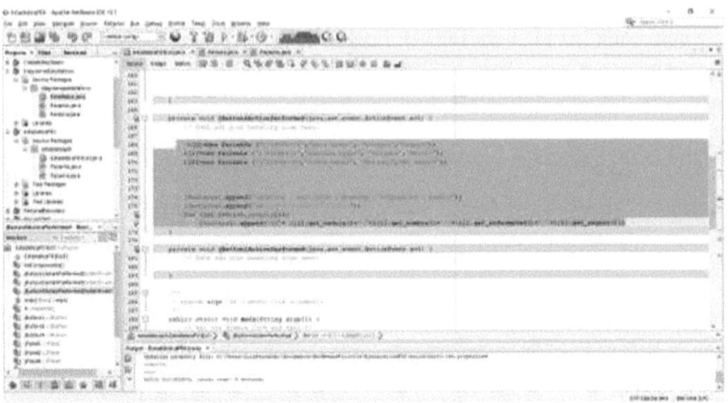

- We create the following functions to draw a bar and pie diagram

```
public void graphBars(Graphics t, Patient A[],int x, int y) {
int contS=0,contC=0,a=20,ancho=40;
for(int i=0;i<A.length;i++)
{
if(A[i].get_insurance().equals("Insurance")) contS++;
if(A[i].get_secure().equals("Not secure")) contC++;
}
//Axes t.drawLine(x,y,x+300,y);
t.drawLine(x,y,x,y-250);
t.setFont(type1); t.setColor(Color.red);
t.drawString("Type",x+300,y+30);
t.drawString("# Secured",x-100,y-250);
//Legend t.setColor(Color.black);
t.drawRect(x+250,y-190,160,100);
t.setFont(type1);
t.setColor(Color.red);
t.drawString("Legend",x+270,y-170);
t.setColor(Color.blue);
t.fillRect(x+270,y-150,width,width/2);
t.setColor(Color.cyan);
t.fillRect(x+270,y-120,width,width/2);
t.setColor(Color.black);
t.drawRect(x+270,y-150,width,width/2);
t.drawRect(x+270,y-120,width,width/2);
t.setFont(type2);
t.drawString("Sure",x+320,y-135);
t.drawString("Not Sure",x+320,y-105);
//Sure t.setColor(Color.blue);
t.fillRect(x+50,y-(contS* a),width,contS*a);
t.setColor(Color.black);
```

* Having:

```
t.drawRect(x+50,y-(contS*a),width,contS*a);
t.drawLine(x,y-(contS*a),x+50+width,y-(contS*a)); t.setFont(type2);
t.drawString("Sure",x+50,y+30);
t.drawString(""+contS,x-20,y-(contS*a));
//Not Sure t.setColor(Color.cyan);
t.fillRect(x+140,y-(contC*a),width,contC*a);
t.setColor(Color.black);
t.drawRect(x+140,y-(contC*a),width,contC*a);
t.drawLine(x+50+width,y-(contC*a),x+140+width,y-(contC*a));
t.setFont(type2);
t.drawString("Not Sure",x+140,y+30);
t.drawString(""+contC,x-20,y-(contC*a));
}
public void graphPastel(Graphics g, int x, int y)
{
int ptot=0; int s=0, ns=0; for(int i=0;i<A.length;i++)
{
if(A[i].get_insurance().equals("Insurance")) s++;
if(A[i].get_secure().equals("Not secure")) ns++;
}
ptot=A.length;
if(ptot!=0){
g.drawRect(x+200,y+20,100,100);
g.drawString("Legend:",x+210,y+40);
g.drawString("S "+(double)(s*100/ptot)+" %",x+230,y+60);
g.drawString("NS "+(double)(ns*100/ptot)+" %",x+230,y+80);
g.drawRect(x+210,y+50,10,10); g.drawRect(x+210,y+70,10,10);
g.fillOval(x-3,y-3,156,156);
g.setColor(new Color(128,0,128));
g.fillArc(x,y,150,150,0,(int)(s*360/ptot));
g.fillRect(x+210,y+50,10,10);
g.setColor(new Color(14,45,34));
g.fillArc(x,y,150,150,(int)(s*360/ptot),(int)(ns*360/ptot));
g.fillRect(x+210,y+70,10,10);
}
}
```

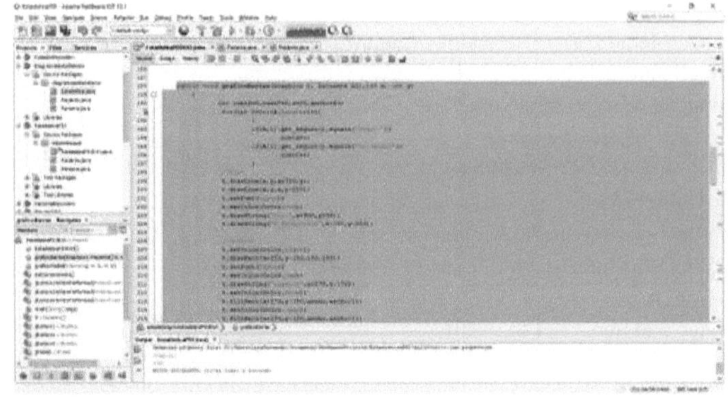

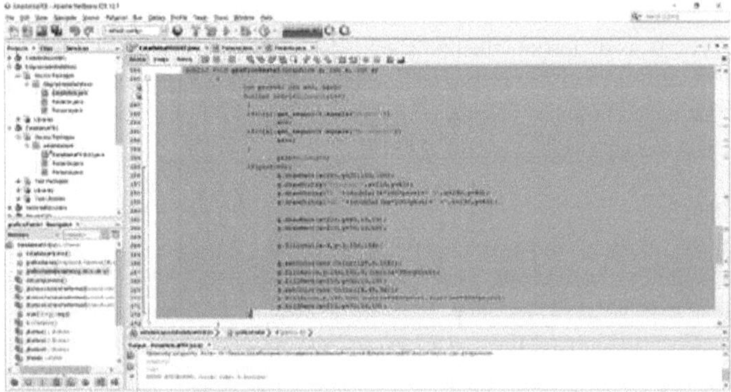

"Now double click on the following button

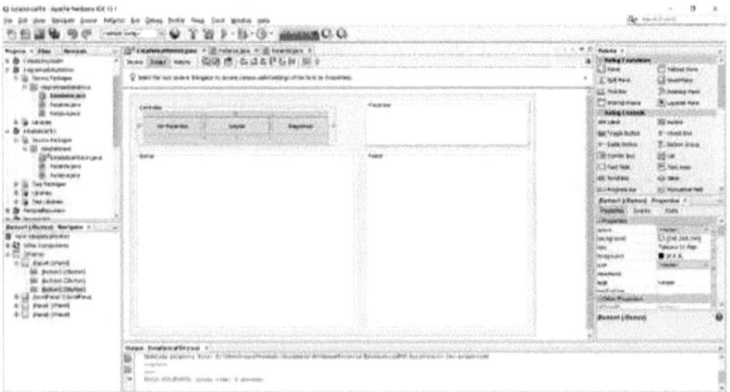

We place the following code:

jTextArea1.setText("");

Having:

"Now double click on the following button

We place the following code graphBars(jPanel1.getGraphics(),A,100,300); graphPastel(jPanel2.getGraphics(),50,125);

- Having:

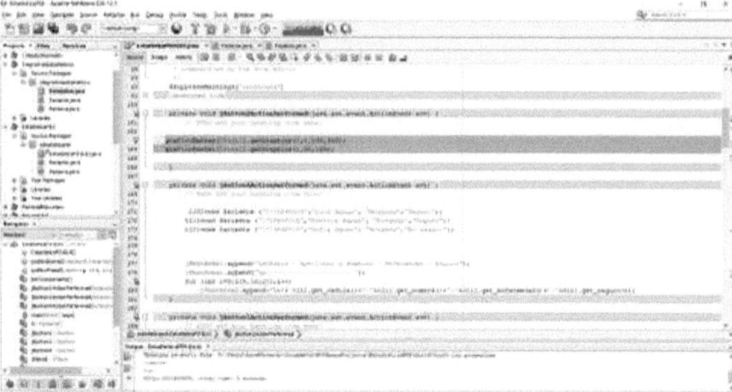

- Compile and run

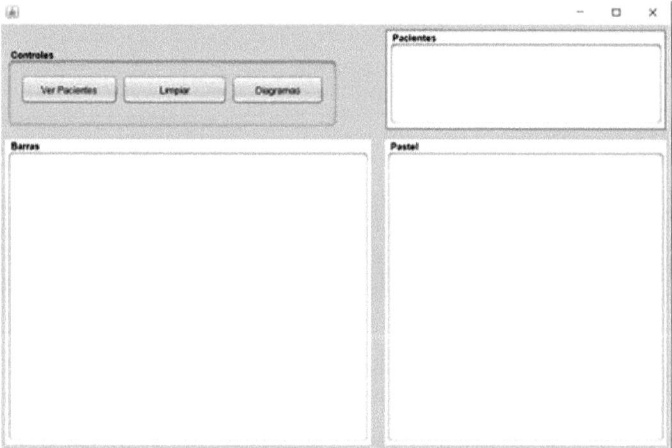

"Click on see patients

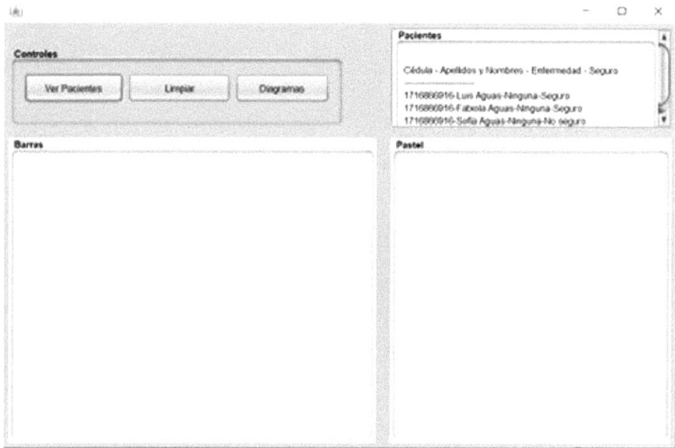

"Then click on Diagrams

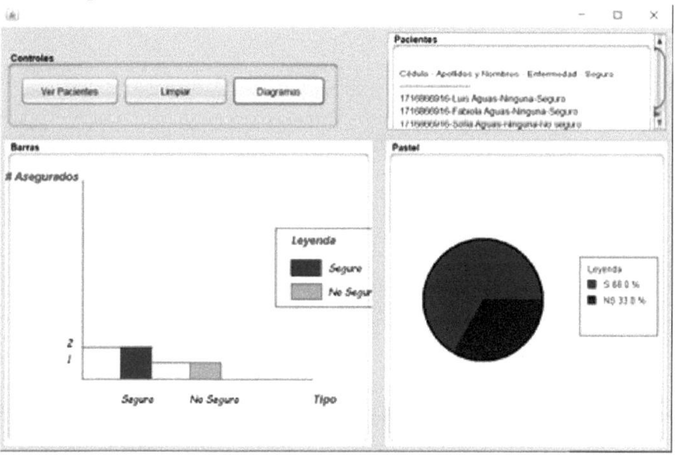

6. BIBLIOGRAPHY:

- Deitel, P., & Deitel, H. (2017). Java: How to Program (10th ed.). Pearson.
- Eckel, B. (2017). Thinking in Java (4th ed.). Prentice Hall.
- Flanagan, D. (2018). Java in a Nutshell: A Desktop Quick Reference (7th ed.). O'Reilly Media.
- Friesen, J. (2019). Java Programming for Beginners. Independently published.
- Gaddis, T. (2018). Starting Out with Java: Early Objects (6th ed.). Pearson.
- Horstmann, C. S. (2019). Core Java, Volume I: Fundamentals (12th ed.). Pearson.
- Liang, Y. D. (2019). Introduction to Java Programming and Data Structures (12th ed.). Pearson.
- Schilde, M. (2016). Java 8 in Action: Lambdas, Streams, and Functional-Style Programming. Manning Publications.
- Sharan, M. (2017). NetBeans: The Definitive Guide (2nd ed.). O'Reilly Media.
- Sierra, K., & Bates, B. (2020). Head First Java (3rd ed.). O'Reilly Media.

Printed by Books on Demand GmbH, Norderstedt / Germany